REVISITING
JOHN GRISHAM

Critical Companions to Popular Contemporary Writers

Second Series

Isabel Allende *by Karen Castellucci Cox*

Julia Alvarez *by Silvio Sirias*

Rudolfo A. Anaya *by Margarite Fernandez Olmos*

Maya Angelou *by Mary Jane Lupton*

Margaret Atwood *by Nathalie Cooke*

Ray Bradbury *by Robin Anne Reid*

Revisiting Mary Higgins Clark *by Linda De Roche*

Louise Erdrich *by Lorena L. Stookey*

Ernest J. Gaines *by Karen Carmean*

Gabriel García Márquez *by Rubén Pelayo*

Kaye Gibbons *by Mary Jean DeMarr*

John Irving *by Josie P. Campbell*

Garrison Keillor *by Marcia Songer*

Jamaica Kincaid *by Lizabeth Paravisini-Gebert*

Revisiting Stephen King *by Sharon A. Russell*

Barbara Kingsolver *by Mary Jean DeMarr*

Maxine Hong Kingston *by E. D. Huntley*

Ursula K. Le Guin *by Susan M. Bernardo and Graham J. Murphy*

Terry McMillan *by Paulette Richards*

Larry McMurtry *by John M. Reilly*

Toni Morrison *by Missy Dehn Kubitschek*

Walter Mosley *by Charles E. Wilson, Jr.*

Gloria Naylor *by Charles E. Wilson, Jr.*

Tim O'Brien *by Patrick A.Smith*

James Patterson *by Joan G. Kotker*

Chaim Potok *by Sanford Sternlicht*

Amy Tan *by E. D. Huntley*

Scott Turow *by Andrew Macdonald and Gina Macdonald*

Anne Tyler *by Paul Bail*

Leon Uris *by Kathleen Shine Cain*

Kurt Vonnegut *by Thomas F. Marvin*

Alice Walker *by Gerri Bates*

James Welch *by Mary Jane Lupton*

Tom Wolfe *by Brian Abel Ragen*

REVISITING JOHN GRISHAM

A Critical Companion

Mary Beth Pringle

CRITICAL COMPANIONS TO POPULAR CONTEMPORARY WRITERS
Kathleen Gregory Klein, Series Editor

Greenwood Press
Westport, Connecticut • London

Library of Congress Cataloging-in-Publication Data

Pringle, Mary Beth, 1943–
　Revisiting John Grisham : a critical companion / Mary Beth Pringle.
　　p. cm. — (Critical companions to popular contemporary writers, ISSN 1082-4979)
　Includes bibliographical references and index.
　ISBN-13: 978–0–313–32335–5 (alk. paper)
　ISBN-10: 0–313–32335–6 (alk. paper)
　1. Grisham, John — Criticism and interpretation. 2. Legal stories, American—History and criticism. I. Title.
PS3557.R5355Z85　2007
813'.54—dc22　　　2007008164

British Library Cataloguing in Publication Data is available.

Library of Congress Catalog Card Number: 2007008164
ISBN-13: 978–0–313–32335–5
ISBN-10: 0–313–32335–6
ISSN: 1082–4979

First published in 2007

Greenwood Press, 88 Post Road West, Westport, CT 06881
An imprint of Greenwood Publishing Group, Inc.
www.greenwood.com

Printed in the United States of America

The paper used in this book complies with the Permanent Paper Standard issued by the National Information Standards Organization (Z39.48–1984).

10　9　8　7　6　5　4　3　2　1

To John Grisham: *who gave us the words.*

Contents

Series Foreword *by Kathleen Gregory Klein*   ix

Acknowledgments   xiii

Introduction   xv

1. Biography of John Grisham   1

2. *The Partner* (1997)   7

3. *The Street Lawyer* (1998)   19

4. *The Testament* (1999)   31

5. *The Brethren* (2000)   45

6. *A Painted House* (2000)   59

7. *Skipping Christmas* (2001)   75

8. *The Summons* (2002)   85

9. *The King of Torts* (2003)   99

10. Recent Books by John Grisham   111

viii <u>Contents</u>

Bibliography 119

Index 129

Series Foreword

The authors who appear in the series Critical Companions to Popular Contemporary Writers are all best-selling writers. They do not simply have one successful novel, but a string of them. Fans, critics, and specialist readers eagerly anticipate their next book. For some, high cash advances and breakthrough sales figures are automatic; movie deals often follow. Some writers become household names, recognized by almost everyone.

But, their novels are read one by one. Each reader chooses to start and, more importantly, to finish a book because of what she or he finds there. The real test of a novel is in the satisfaction its readers experience. This series acknowledges the extraordinary involvement of readers and writers in creating a best-seller.

The authors included in this series were chosen by an Advisory Board composed of high school English teachers and high school and public librarians. They ranked a list of best-selling writers according to their popularity among different groups of readers. For the first series, writers in the top-ranked group who had received no book-length, academic, literary analysis (or none in at least the past ten years) were chosen. Because of this selection method, Critical Companions to Popular Contemporary Writers meets a need that is being addressed nowhere else. The success of these volumes as reported by reviewers, librarians, and teachers led to an expansion of the series mandate to include some writers with wide critical attention—Toni Morrison, John Irving, and Maya Angelou, for example—to extend the usefulness of the series.

The volumes in the series are written by scholars with particular expertise in analyzing popular fiction. These specialists add an academic focus to the popular success that these writers already enjoy. The series is designed to appeal to a wide range of readers. The general reading public will find explanations for the appeal of these well-known writers. Fans will find biographical and fictional questions answered. Students will find literary analysis, discussions of fictional genres, care-fully organized introductions to new ways of reading the novels, and bibliographies for additional research. Whether browsing through the book for pleasure or using it for an assignment, readers will find that the most recent novels of the authors are included.

Each volume begins with a biographical chapter drawing on published information, autobiographies or memoirs, prior interviews, and, in some cases, interviews given especially for this series. A chapter on literary history and genres describes how the author's work fits into a larger literary context. The following chapters analyze the writer's most important, most popular, and most recent novels in detail. Each chapter focuses on one or more novels. This approach, suggested by the Advisory Board as the most useful to student research, allows for an in-depth analysis of the writer's fiction. Close and careful readings with numerous examples show readers exactly how the novels work. These chapters are organized around three central elements: plot development (how the story line moves forward), character development (what the reader knows of the important figures), and theme (the significant ideas of the novel). Chapters may also include sections on generic conventions (how the novel is similar or different from others in its same category of science fiction, fantasy, thriller, etc.), narrative point of view (who tells the story and how), symbols and literary language, and historical or social context. Each chapter ends with an "alternative reading" of the novel. The volume concludes with a primary and secondary bibliography, including reviews.

The alternative readings are a unique feature of this series. By demonstrating a particular way of reading each novel, they provide a clear example of how a specific perspective can reveal important aspects of the book. In the alternative reading sections, one contemporary literary theory—way of reading, such as feminist criticism, Marxism, new historicism, deconstruction, or Jungian psychological critique—is defined in brief, easily comprehensible language. That definition is then applied to the novel to highlight specific features that might go unnoticed or be understood differently in a more general reading. Each volume defines two or three specific theories, making them part of the reader's understanding of how diverse meanings may be constructed from a single novel.

Taken collectively, the volumes in the Critical Companions to Popular Contemporary Writers series provide a wide-ranging investigation of the complexities of current best-selling fiction. By treating these novels seriously as both literary works and publishing successes, the series demonstrates the potential of popular literature in contemporary culture.

Kathleen Gregory Klein
Southern Connecticut State University

Acknowledgments

My thanks to Wright State University's College of Liberal Arts for a research grant and to Robin McNamara, student in the department of English, for his help gathering materials for this book.

Introduction

If author Nathaniel Hawthorne were writing in the twenty-first century instead of the nineteenth, he would have John Grisham to complain about instead of that "damn mob of scribbling women" who regularly outsold him. Regardless of whether Grisham ranks first, he is surely among the top-selling writers of the past 20 years, maybe even of the twentieth-century. Estimating the number of books he has sold would quickly date this introduction. Like McDonald's hamburgers sold, the number rises quickly. And he's not just an American writer; he is an international phenomenon, with readers in Beirut and Belfast consuming his words as avidly as those in Buffalo and Boise. In fact, individual Grisham titles have been translated into more than 35 languages and have sold well into the millions of copies around the world.

This volume, *Revisiting John Grisham: A Critical Companion,* is a follow-up to *John Grisham: A Critical Companion,* published by Greenwood in 1997. The earlier work examined Grisham's first six novels, *A Time to Kill* (1989) through *The Rainmaker* (1995), with a shortened discussion of *The Runaway Jury* (1996). It looked also at the legal thriller genre, at its ancestors and descendents, and, briefly, at Grisham's life. *Revisiting John Grisham* picks up where *John Grisham: A Critical Companion* left off. It updates the Grisham biography and covers Grisham's next eight works, beginning with *The Partner,* published in 1997, and ending with *The King of Torts,* appearing in

2003. A final chapter (chapter 10) briefly discusses Grisham's publications since 2003: novels *Bleachers* (2003), *The Last Juror* (2004), and *The Broker* (2005), and a nonfiction effort called *The Innocent Man* (2006).

As to the organization of *Revisiting John Grisham,* the book's main chapters cover one novel at a time. Each begins with a look at the book's publication history and plot. Next comes analysis of character and plot development, social and literary contexts, thematic issues, and key reviews, all presented in a straightforward and accessible style.

The intended audiences of *Revisiting John Grisham* are those who read Grisham's books for enlightenment and pure pleasure, as well as high school and college students who have been assigned a Grisham novel. That popular works such as Grisham's are being taught serves as evidence of their literary significance. And they *are* well worth reading. After all, the rules of plot development, characterization, and theme that govern the creation of a thriller are the same rules that govern more thematically complex fictional works. *Revisiting John Grisham* accords Grisham's novels the same respectful analysis one would give to any classic text. It assumes that all novels—genre and otherwise—grow out of a social and literary context and that each affords readers important information and a satisfying engagement with words.

As the author of *Revisiting John Grisham,* I am mindful that Grisham despises literary reviewers and reviews. He once said in a 1997 interview with bookreporter.com that "I have learned not to read the reviews. Period. And I hate reviewers. All of them, or at least all but two or three. Life is much simpler ignoring reviews and the nasty people who write them. Critics should find meaningful work." Even a cursory look at newspaper evaluations of Grisham's novels helps explain his rancor. It must be tiresome having your best seller publicly sniped at by those who often have not written a book themselves and who seem to enjoy lambasting what other readers clearly delight in. That said, I still believe that evaluating popular fiction, Grisham's works included, is important and ultimately respectful. Doing so serves as a reminder that what we consider highbrow fiction and popular fiction are more alike than they are different. Besides, postmodernism and, in particular, postmodern literary criticism have done much to break down barriers between so-called levels of fiction, occasionally showing detective and romance novels as well as fantasy fiction to be subtly epistemological texts.

In writing *Revisiting John Grisham,* I have tried to be evenhanded in treating Grisham's books and critics' evaluations of them. Sometimes those who review novels let personal biases or a wicked sense of humor override fair-mindedness. Nevertheless, there is often something of value in reviews, even snide ones, and so opinions of every stripe are offered here, including my own, and readers are free to assess the validity and tone of those opinions for themselves.

As *Revisiting John Grisham* and *John Grisham: A Critical Companion* firmly attest, Grisham continues to amass a remarkable literary corpus. Although legal thrillers are his forte, he ranges widely within and sometimes beyond the genre, telling stories that are close to his heart. Judging from the size of his audiences, his stories are close to readers' hearts as well.

What might explain his popularity, the steadfast loyalty of his readers? Maybe the answer to these questions lies in the moral vision that underpins each of his books. Grisham vehemently maintains, especially in his early works, a worldview that is reminiscent of those detective novels found in the "cozy" tradition popular during the first half of the twentieth century. Like the cozy writers, Grisham depicts an essentially orderly and moral world gone temporarily awry when someone commits a crime. In Grisham's first six thrillers, a lawyer sees to it that wrong is righted and order is restored. In his later works, that same process usually—sometimes partially—occurs, even though his protagonists are not as instrumental as his earlier ones in fixing what is broken.

In a 1992 *USA Today* interview, Grisham said he wrote things he wouldn't be embarrassed to have his mother read. He was apparently referring to the absence of sex and bloody violence in his books; however, more subtle issues of propriety and reassurance in his writing may explain his great popularity. In Grisham's works, fictional and otherwise, the bad guys are generally brought down or at least shown to be the thugs and wastrels they are. Good guys do the right thing, or Grisham makes clear to readers what the right thing is.

Good people, according to Grisham, exhibit generosity, a strong sense of purpose, moral responsibility, empathy, and kindness. A good world is one in which such qualities either win out or show themselves to be positive. Grisham's first six novels ensure that readers meet such protagonists and visit such worlds. Except for 1997's *The Partner*, the novels from *A Time to Kill* (1989) through *The Street Lawyer* (1998) tell the stories of comparatively uncomplicated heroes who valiantly strive to correct problems in their flawed environments. In *A Time to Kill*, Jake Brigance achieves justice for African American Carl Lee Hailey after white men rape Hailey's daughter. In *The Firm*, Mitch McDeere defeats the immoral microcosmic world of the law firm Bendini, Lambert, & Locke. *The Pelican Brief*'s Darby Shaw protects endangered wildlife against the evil land baron,

Victor Mattiece. Reggie Love in *The Client* saves little Mark Sway from his would-be killers, and together, they close a mafia-owned toxic dump. In *The Chamber,* Adam Hall does everything he can to rescue his grandfather from the gas chamber, not because his grandfather is innocent of the crime for which he was convicted, a KKK-inspired bombing, but because in Grisham's universe, capital punishment is quite simply wrong. Rudy Baylor, a soon-to-graduate law student in *The Rainmaker,* represents leukemic Donny Black against the megalith insurance company unwilling to pay for a lifesaving bone-marrow transplant. Juror Nicholas Easter in *The Runaway Jury* refuses to let a tobacco company, Pynex, off the hook when its product kills a 51-year-old smoker. And in *The Street Lawyer,* Michael Brock quits his job when he learns the law firm he works for profits from the improper and illegal evictions of poor people from their Washington, D.C., apartments. In each case, the novel's protagonist acts with moral conviction in bringing down wrongdoers. The assumption is that order has been restored by way of a hero's right actions.

That is not to say, however, that Grisham's early heroes are perfect people who lead exemplary lives. Jake Brigance in *A Time to Kill* drinks a fair amount and flirts with female colleagues and waitresses. Mitch McDeere in *The Firm* is unfaithful to his wife, and Darby Shaw in *The Pelican Brief* is alienated from her family. *The Client*'s Reggie Love is a recovering alcoholic who lost custody of her children in a divorce, and Rudy Baylor in *The Runaway Jury* is something of an academic dud. Nevertheless, Grisham portrays all these early heroes as good if flawed people, eager or at least willing to defend the powerless who are in trouble. As I have written elsewhere, "They are romantics who see themselves as champions of the underdog, as principled practitioners within the justice system or as outcasts because the system itself is flawed." They are an endearing lot for these reasons.

However, beginning in 1997, Grisham's legal-thriller heroes and the worlds they inhabit gradually began taking a slightly darker turn. Patrick Lanigan in *The Partner* (1977) started the trend. Readers try to figure out whether he is somewhat flawed or thoroughly reprehensible, after learning that he has stolen $90 million from the law office where he worked and has placed the money in foreign bank accounts only he can access. He then fakes his death in an automobile accident. By disappearing, he can, he hopes, keep the money for himself.

Even though Grisham works hard in the rest of the novel to extricate Lanigan from the *appearance* of impropriety, he is never completely successful. Regardless of the legality involved in Lanigan's taking money that doesn't belong to him, what kind of man fabricates a grizzly car crash, complete with metal carnage and a bloody corpse? What kind of man washes his hands of a daughter he has parented because DNA tests show she is not biologically his? Even though *The Partner*'s plot eventually reveals that Lanigan may have good reasons for seizing the cash, he remains a tainted character, not someone Grisham is able (or wants?) to completely redeem.

Nor is Josh Stafford in *The Testament* as admirable as earlier Grisham heroes. A recovering alcoholic and drug addict of the white-knuckles variety, he tries to maintain his sobriety through extensive and not always successful efforts. Although his journeys into the Amazon to find the heiress Rachel Lane help him attain a more settled and peaceful life, readers are unsure at novel's end whether he will be able to stay sober or whether he has thoroughly reformed his life.

The Brethren does not offer a better-behaved hero; in fact, it offers no hero at all. Presidential candidate Aaron Lake is hardly admirable; he is dishonest with others and with himself, surreptitiously entering correspondence with a young gay man while publicly presenting himself as a grieving heterosexual widower. In fact, Grisham depicts Lake as somewhat robotic, except for his clandestine letter writing, acting only when directed to do so by Teddy Maynard, the CIA boss who has engineered his candidacy. The three "brethren" of the novel's title are hardly heroic either. Imprisoned for assorted crimes, they spend their days scamming others out of their money and self-respect.

Although Ray Atlee in *The Summons* is not a bad person, he is not like Grisham's early heroes either. As with Patrick Lanigan, Atlee opts for quick riches, and people are injured or even die so that he can have a chance to keep the $3 million he uncovers in his deceased father's study. *The King of Torts*' Clay Carter is equally vulnerable to greed, deserting the public defenders' office to practice a get-rich-quick legal specialty, mass tort litigation, and eventually committing illegal acts of insider trading. The desire to accumulate wealth quickly subsumes any of his more positive character traits. Unlike Clay Carter, who spends his early career in the public defender's office and then sells out, *The Broker*'s Joel Backman has a long history of sleazy behavior. He wants only to save his own life, which hardly puts him in the same league as the brave Darby Shaw or the hardworking Jake Brigance, who labor on behalf of selfless causes.

The nature of evil also changes between Grisham's early and later works. In his first six novels, Grisham depicts focused, momentary evil, much like that in the cozy mysteries where murder is an aberration in an otherwise orderly world. In *A Time To Kill*, two bad men rape a little

African American girl, but there are plenty of upstanding citizens such as Jake Brigance and the child's father who see that wrong is punished and order restored. In *The Firm* and *The Street Lawyer*, evil occurs within the walls of law firms, and the right-thinking attorneys who find out about it provide a form of correction. In *The Pelican Brief* and *The Client*, evil is manifested by the few who would harm wildlife or poison the land, and in *The Chamber* and *The Street Lawyer*, evil exists in the hearts of those who lack empathy for others' suffering. Grisham also targets corporate greed—in *The Rainmaker* the greed of a medical insurance company and in *The Runaway Jury* the greed of a large tobacco firm. In each case, strong voices oppose the actions of the few, and evil is contained.

Beginning with *The Partner*, however, greed often lurks in the heart of the protagonist himself, the person who earlier in Grisham's corpus would have stood in opposition to wrongdoing. Patrick Lanigan's motive for disappearing is to get and stay rich. Troy Phelan, the consummately selfish billionaire industrialist in *The Testament*, is dead after the first few pages, and Josh Stafford, whose alcoholic history shows he has always tended first to his own needs, takes on the daunting task of locating Phelan's missing beneficiary. To be sure, his actions are profit-driven. Only Rachel Lane in *The Testament* behaves well. Although she chooses the life of a missionary, rejecting the trappings of the flawed world she grew up in, her admirable behavior is not the focus of the novel.

Greed and selfishness permeate *The Brethren*, and there is no one to combat or counter their effects. All the novel's key characters hunger to have or control something: Aaron Lake wants power and perhaps the risks of casual sex, the Brethren want to scam the world, and Teddy Maynard would control the executive branch of the U.S. government.

Sudden temptation in the form of windfall profits lures Ray Atlee in *The Summons* and Patrick Lanigan in *The Partner* into desperate situations. Both novels focus on protagonists keeping money that is illegitimately theirs, instead of on heroes wanting to restore money to its rightful owners. Grisham questions the characters of both men, as well as that of Clay Carter in *King of Torts* and Joel Backman in *The Broker*. One wonders whether this shift in plotting reflects a change in Grisham's thinking about evil in the world, or whether success has given him the freedom to depict the world as he has always really seen it. Regardless, Grisham makes clear, even in these later works, what is right behavior and what is wrong, regardless of whether his protagonists are themselves able to act admirably.

Besides evil in the world, certain topics and themes permeate Grisham's writing, first novel to last. His principal characters, for example, suffer to one degree or another the effects of isolation, even though many of them have sought it out. Judging from Grisham's fiction, readers could easily conclude that the author feels both drawn to and repelled by the solitary life. He presents connection with others as problematic, but ultimately as our salvation.

Another issue that has continued to interest Grisham is capital punishment. He has treated it in *The Chamber* (1994), *The Last Juror* (2004), and now *The Innocent Man* (2006). In all three, Grisham speaks strongly and persuasively against the barbaric practice of taking an eye for an eye, a life for a life. In both *The Last Juror* and *The Innocent Man,* the convicted individual is eventually found to be innocent. But the possibility of executing the wrong person is not Grisham's only reason for objecting to the practice. Sam Cayhall is indeed guilty of murder in *The Chamber,* but Grisham insists that, by definition, the death penalty is cruel and inhumane, that for him it violates some key moral covenant.

Rape is also treated in three of Grisham's books: in his first, *A Time to Kill* (1989); his seventeenth, *The Last Juror* (2004); and his latest, *The Innocent Man* (2006). Grisham apparently considers it an act of consummate evil. It is especially despicable in *A Time to Kill,* where the victim is a child, and in *The Last Juror,* where children witness the unspeakably violent attack against their mother.

Although Grisham's two early female heroes, Darby Shaw and Reggie Love, are wonderfully positive characters, women and marriage tend to take a big hit in Grisham's writing. His later novels especially are littered with angry females and broken male–female relationships. In the early thrillers, wives like Clare Brigance in *A Time to Kill* and Abby McDeere in *The Firm* adore their husbands and are hugely tolerant of male misbehavior. Clare conveniently leaves town so that Jake can work with Ellen, an attractive Ole Miss law student, in preparing murderer Carl Lee Hailey's defense. Mitch McDeere's wife Abby in *The Firm* sticks by her husband even after he commits adultery. She also helps him gather evidence against his former law firm colleagues. Rudy Baylor's girlfriend Kelly loyally supports Rudy's efforts to save Donny Black in *The Rainmaker.* The only other positively portrayed females with roles large enough to mention are Miss Callie Ruffin in *The Last Juror* and Francesca Ferro in *The Broker.* Because Miss Callie is elderly, she does not pose a sexual threat to the protagonist, which may explain her lovable characterization. Francesca Ferro is seemingly the only person in *The Broker* not trying to kill Joel Backman, but theirs is a comparatively new, and therefore untested, relationship.

In the rest of Grisham's thrillers, women embody vapidity or evil shrewdness. As well, they are disloyal and sexually predatory. Trudy, in

The Partner, for example, takes on boyfriend Lance, "a hold-over from high school," while still married to Patrick Lanigan, and the child she has said is Patrick's is not biologically his at all (46). Assuming a new identity in Brazil as Danilo Silva, Patrick meets Eva Miranda, a beautiful female attorney. The novel implicitly asks, however, whether he can trust Eva any more than he could Trudy. In *The Street Lawyer,* Michael Brock's wife responds to his negligent treatment of her by going to medical school and becoming as work-obsessed as her husband. Somehow though, Grisham appears to hold her more responsible than Michael for the breakup of their marriage, and he casts her in a more negative light overall. Nate O'Riley's wife in *The Testament* has long since dumped him, and Troy Phelan has numerous ex-spouses. The Phelan exes, caricatured by Grisham, are consummately shallow and materialistic. In *The Brethren,* Aaron Lake's wife is dead. The brethren's wives are barely mentioned except that Finn Yarber's is said to have "a grey butch cut and hair under her arms," a particularly dismissive snapshot (97). The few women mentioned in *The Summons* include Claudia Gates, who was Ray Atlee's father's mistress and who is depicted as nice enough but not particularly smart, and a couple of female students who flirt with Ray, their law school professor. Clay Carter in *King of Torts* has a vapid girlfriend who marries someone with money because her parents disapprove of her relationship with Ray. Then, inexplicably, she has a complete turnaround, divorcing that man because he works too hard and declaring Clay her one true love. There is also the puzzling, ambiguous portrait in *The Chamber* of Adam Hall's Aunt Lee, who, though significantly older than he is, seems more like a date than a doting relative. Although Rachel Lane, the heiress in *The Testament,* might be seen to compensate for these negative portrayals of women, she is wholly otherworldly, an image of goodness rather than a real person.

Females in Grisham's non-thrillers are more positively portrayed than the women in his legal thrillers. Both the mother and grandmother in *A Painted House* are life-giving, nurturing, gentle, and idealistic. Even so, Tally Spruill, something of a vixen, skirts the edges of little Luke Chandler's world. Nora Krank in *Skipping Christmas* tolerates her husband's cranky behavior and also manages to do the right thing for her daughter and her daughter's new fiancé.

Despite their solitary natures, some of Grisham's male main characters prioritize male friends (always lawyers) over marriage or other intimate partnerships. Three cases in point are Jake Brigance's relationship with drinking buddy and former law partner Lucien Wilbanks in *A Time to Kill,* Michael Brock's developing friendship with street lawyer Mordecai

Green in *The Street Lawyer,* and Ray Atlee's bond with his father's friend, Harry Rex Varner, in *The Summons.* Grisham's writings show that loyalty and sociability, as a link between same-sex friends, are strong personal values for Grisham.

Like his legal thrillers and new nonfiction book, Grisham's non-thrillers stress the importance of connectedness and community. All three—*A Painted House, Skipping Christmas,* and *Bleachers*—present characters who feel the effects of exclusion or isolation in their lives and the need for group solidarity. Family and friendship are as important in Black Oak, Arkansas *(A Painted House)*, and in Messina, Mississippi *(Bleachers)*, Grisham shows, as they are in Bologna, Italy *(The Broker)*. Devoted service to others is as prized.

Grisham has traveled in recent years, and his affection for new places shows up in his books. One wonders where Grisham will travel next in real life and whether that place will become the setting of a future novel. Another possibility, of course, is that he will continue to set new works in beautiful Brazil and Italy.

With 19 books available to readers in bookstores, libraries, and online, Grisham shows no signs of slowing down. He has said he will write until he gets tired of the process. So far, his prodigious output amounts to a book or two a year. If his readers are lucky, he is already plotting his next novel and preparing to withdraw to his study to write it down. We want to be told stories. And millions of people enthusiastically consider John Grisham their favorite storyteller.

1

Biography of John Grisham

In a 2001 interview on National Public Radio, John Grisham conceded that *A Painted House* says a lot about his own childhood. Grisham set this novel in northeastern Arkansas near the small town of Black Oak, where Grisham himself spent his first seven years. Grisham's descriptions of the region, of the farm where his seven-year-old protagonist, Luke, lives, and of the cotton harvests are all vividly written.

As Grisham makes clear in *A Painted House*, life was hard. Elsewhere he says, "I'm not going to say it was a sad life, but it was one that we put behind us quickly and we left as soon as we could. . . . It took my father, I think, about ten years to pay off all of his debts. . . . And we were very happy to be off the farm because the work was brutal and it was sort of a grim and dreary way to make a living, especially when you weren't making a living" (Wertheimer). According to Grisham, the sad memories haven't waned. When his parents visit Black Oak, "they are almost always a little depressed . . . because it brings back such painful memories of farming and losing everything" (Wertheimer).

Even so, as *A Painted House* shows, shared family activities helped soften what was otherwise a difficult life. Grisham notes that baseball games such as the one between the Black Oak Baptists and Methodists really happened, although he doesn't say whether his grandfather, similar to Luke's, refused to shake hands with the Methodists when they won.

Apparently, Grisham's family, like Luke's, listened to St. Louis Cardinal baseball games while sitting together on their farmhouse's front porch.

A Painted House may be as close as readers get to an account of Grisham's early life; details are scarce and superficial. He was born in Jonesboro, Arkansas, he and former-president Bill Clinton are distant cousins, and his father was a construction worker and frequently moved the family. He dreamed of becoming a professional baseball player, and his mother, a housewife, made sure the young Grisham always had a library card. In an interview with *The Book Report,* Grisham confirmed that he read a lot, mentioning as favorites "Dr. Seuss, the Hardy Boys, Emil and the Detectives, Chip Hilton, and lots of Mark Twain and Dickens" (Kornbluth).

Information about the next stage of Grisham's life is equally scarce: He earned a D in freshman composition, had a college major in accounting, and went to law school at the University of Mississippi with plans to become a tax attorney. After graduation he practiced criminal law for a while and then civil law, enjoying neither. In response to an interview question—"What was most satisfying about the law?"—Grisham answered, "Getting out of it" (Kornbluth).

Grisham ran for the Mississippi legislature in 1983 and won, but quit before the end of his second term. He felt, he said, that it was impossible to change much as a lawmaker. It was during this time that Grisham began writing novels. He wrote his first, *A Time to Kill,* early in the mornings before heading off to work. Published in June 1988, it had a modest printing of 5,000 copies and sold poorly.

Grisham's public biography credits his second novel, *The Firm,* with turning what was a "hobby into a new full-time career" (www.randomhouse. com/features/grisham/main.php). A thriller about a young lawyer courted and hired by "an apparently perfect law firm that was not what it appeared," *The Firm* was a mega-success (Grisham Web site). Grisham sold the film rights for $600,000, and thus began his career as a best-selling writer of legal thrillers. Since the publication of *A Time to Kill* and *The Firm,* Grisham has published another 17 books, most of which have achieved number one status on the *New York Times* best-seller list.

As of this writing, Grisham and his wife, Renee, live on a plantation near Charlottesville, Virginia. They also keep a Victorian farmhouse near Oxford, Mississippi. Grisham enjoys a "close editorial collaboration" with his wife. He says, "she has an uncanny ability to spot a good story; I tend to think that almost anything will work. Once I start writing, she is merciless as the chapters pour forth. She enjoys picking a good brawl over a subplot, a weak character, an unnecessary scene. I accuse her of looking for trouble—and, inevitably, I return to the typewriter and fix whatever troubles her" (Kornbluth). Grisham and Renee have a grown son and daughter, Ty and Shea. Ty reportedly enjoys baseball as much as his father and has played on his college teams at the University of Virginia.

In 1996 Grisham stopped writing long enough to honor "a commitment made before he had retired from the law to become a full-time writer: representing the family of a railroad brakeman killed when he was pinned between two cars." He was successful in winning his clients $683,500, "the biggest verdict of his career" (Grisham Web site). Afterward, he was "thrilled to leave the courtroom," and when asked whether he'd ever try another case, Grisham responded, "I can't see myself returning. Trial work is quite stressful when you do it every day, and I had not seen a courtroom in eight years. Never say never—but never again" (Kornbluth).

Despite his success, Grisham is still the same quietly spiritual person he always was. A "lifelong Baptist," Grisham and his wife have taught Sunday school in their local church. They've also traveled to the northern part of Brazil several times to build medical clinics and homes (Jones 65). They go, according to Grisham, with "church groups, and our mission each trip is to build a small chapel for a local congregation, and also to provide medical care to the sick" (Kornbluth).

As his books indicate, Grisham's Baptist underpinnings cause him to struggle against materialism. In *The Testament*, Grisham's hero, Nate, struggles similarly. About Nate, Grisham writes, "Success had brought him nothing but misery. Success had thrown him in the gutter" (Jones 67). When an interviewer asked Grisham whether "Nate's concerns are his concerns," Grisham hedged. His wife offered a fuller answer: "When you're successful all of a sudden, the way we were, there is a lot of guilt. . . . I think in John's books that he does try to resolve that subconsciously" (Jones 67).

Grisham frequently uses his wealth to help others. As soon as he and his family moved to Charlottesville, Grisham made baseball available to kids who hadn't been able to play before by creating Cove Creek Park. With its six baseball diamonds, clubhouse, and batting cages, the park is a testament to "Grisham's generosity and his determination" (Jones 67).

Additionally, Grisham never forgets those who have helped him. After publishing his first novel, *A Time to Kill*, he went to a friend's bookstore, Square Books in Oxford, Mississippi, and asked if the friend would hold a book signing for him. The friend obliged. Even though he now sells millions of books, Grisham still visits and holds book signings at Square Books and four other bookstores that helped promote his work: Burke's in Memphis;

That Bookstore in Blytheville, Arkansas (Grisham's grandfather once owned a piano store right across the street); Lemuria in Jackson, Mississippi; and Reed's Gum Tree in Tupelo, Mississippi. Rare in the case of someone so successful, Grisham arranges these signings by himself (Summer 33). An old friend says, "He is unfailingly gracious, and his signings are like reunions of old friends" (Summer 33). After Hallmark Hall of Fame's *A Painted House* was filmed near the Blytheville bookstore, locals who appeared in the film showed up there for Grisham's autograph session. In an interview at the time, the store's owner said, "Daily, people are in the store who are in the film, or their relatives are in the film, or their trucks are in the film" (Summer 33). Grisham's family members who live in the area also showed up with the store hosting "luncheons for Grisham's mother and several aunts" (Summer 33).

Signings follow a carefully proscribed procedure. Tickets are given out by time slot to 200 people. Grisham signs his new book for those 200 (no more than two copies each) and then signs the remainder of the bookstore's 3,000-copy order. He also meets with local journalists. After the signing, the bookstore sends signed copies to people across the United States who have placed orders for them (Summer 33). When one store hosted a speaking event instead of a signing, it was televised and syndicated by Mississippi Educational Television. The event was so successful that the bookstore planned more such events for subsequent novels. One event, following publication of *King of Torts*, involved a discussion among Grisham and two popular Mississippi writers: Nevada Barr and Greg Iles (Summer 33).

There are other examples of Grisham's generosity. When an Oxford friend Marc Smirnoff bought the magazine *Oxford American*, and it fell on hard times, Grisham, "a graduate of ole Miss and an Oxford resident, stepped in as benefactor and figurehead publisher, or as Smirnoff calls him, 'angel' and 'godfather'" (Agovino). Together, the two gave the magazine a nudge toward stardom. In 1999 *Oxford American* "captured a prestigious National Magazine Award for its annual Southern music issue, an award that raised eyebrows among the New York magazine–world hegemony" (Agovino). Although Smirnoff and Grisham recently sold the magazine to a media group in Little Rock, Grisham, out of loyalty, has stayed involved in its publication.

Why has Grisham continued to be one of the most popular and successful writers of "the legal thriller the world has ever known"? (Victory 37). One critic says it's because Grisham's heroes get beaten and bruised and "often pay in pain for their beliefs" (Victory 37). Other possibilities are that Grisham's heroes are loners—a trait that appeals to the general public—wrestling with a bigger, tougher foe, or that Grisham works from the assumption that Americans despise slick lawyers.

Grisham's readers trust him. As Richard Victory points out, once any writer succeeds a few times, readers go on autopilot when a new book comes out. They buy someone whom they've read and liked before. For the most part, people don't choose a Grisham novel because of its beautiful language. Instead they willingly trade language for plot. They want to wonder what will happen next, and Grisham responds by surprising them. In short, as Victory says, Grisham feeds the American public's paranoia. His books are filled with murders and murderers, cheaters and those cheated. And in Grisham, some sort of social justice usually wins out in the end.

Finally, according to Victory, people read Grisham because they "admire his humanity." He has compassion for his characters, "particularly those whose birthright wasn't a silver spoon" (37). Many agree with this assessment that Grisham's "instincts as a human are so good that as you read his books you pull for him to be a better writer" (37). Grisham writings, in terms of popular culture, "have come to resemble runic stones around which regular readers and snobs like me gather, hoping for an experience that will magically illuminate a large truth up to now out of sight" (Victory 37).

As for Grisham, he is unfailingly modest about his work. "I don't pretend it's literature," he says. "It's high-quality, professional entertainment" (Jones 65). He is also realistic about the future. "You have some really good years where you're on top, and then one day it's over. I won't always write a book a year. I won't always write about lawyers. Once the legal thrillers run their course, I'd like to get back to telling stories about the South and Ford County" (Jones 65).

Some might consider this an admission that Grisham sees himself as part of the great Southern literary tradition. Not so. "Oh, no. I could have grown up in Denver and written *The Firm*. . . . I think one day I'd like to *become* a Southern writer. . . . Yeah, that's my goal, to become a true Southern writer . . . Who also sells a few copies. In my lifetime" (Jones 65).

Grisham seems to be inching his way in that direction. His 2003 work *Bleachers* is closer to the comparatively lyrical *A Painted House* than it is to the legal thriller genre. Additionally, a March 2005 Doubleday press release announced that Grisham would next write a nonfiction work. That work eventually became *The Innocent Man: Murder and Injustice in a Small Town* (2007). It is about "a death row inmate [Ronald Keith Williamson] exonerated by DNA." According to the release, "Mr. Grisham read his [Williamson's] obituary in *The New York Times,* and found it impossible to forget." Grisham modestly adds, "Not in my most creative hour could I imagine a story as compelling as Ron Williamson's."

Each of Grisham's books takes him about six months to write plus several months of pondering and outlining. "I'll start probably in about June, and I'm doing two or three pages a day. And after Labor Day, once the kids go back to school and, you know, summer's over, I sort of go in a cave and don't come out for two months and do the book. But the whole process—I mean, even now I'm making notes for the next book; I'm thinking about the outline. The actual writing is three hard months and three pretty easy months" (Simon).

Despite all his movement toward other niches, John Grisham remains king of the legal thriller. Along with Scott Turow, he has shaped the legal thriller into a separate and very special genre. Movies have been made of several of his novels, and by 1999, four had been major hits (Jones 65). But Grisham has also been part of the popular literature scene at a time of important changes. Each new Grisham book gets marketed in new ways—and in new places:

> American best sellers are now worldwide best sellers. Grisham has been translated into [at least 34] languages, and he's been a No. 1 best seller in eight countries. Even ones where the legal system is entirely unlike the American model he writes about. And uniquely among that elite club of mega-selling authors, his audience cannot be corralled into a discernible demographic. He sells to everyone, from teens to senior citizens, from lawyers in Biloxi to housewives in Hong Kong. (Jones 65)

2

The Partner (1997)

John Grisham's eighth novel, *The Partner*, debuted on AOL (then short for America Online) as the first major piece of popular fiction to launch prepublication in cyberspace. Chapter 1 appeared on AOL's *The Book Report* on February 12, 1997, two weeks before Doubleday released the hardcover version to bookstores. Chapter 2 followed in the same space five days later. By publication day, February 26, 1997, two hundred thousand people had already read the book's first two chapters and an accompanying interview (Rotenberk 45). Later, as a prelude to the novel's arrival in bookstores, Doubleday gave 65 online retailers the same two chapters and interview, as well as access to an audio clip.

This sales strategy seems to have worked, with *The Partner* quickly springing to the top of the fiction best-seller list. The first printing's 2.8 million copies sold briskly and were distributed as feature selections through the Literary Guild, the Doubleday Book Club, and the Mystery Guild. To ensure high bookstore visibility for the novel, Grisham appeared at the New York City Borders for a lunchtime signing. He also did interviews on *Today*, *Entertainment Tonight*, and NPR's *Fresh Air*. Early reports showed *The Partner* easily keeping up with Grisham's previous novel, *The Runaway Jury*. In fact, *The Partner*'s sales were "1300% higher than the #2 fiction best seller at Barnes and Noble (Dean Koontz's *Sole Survivor*)" (Maryles 18).

THE PLOT

The Partner combines Grisham's usual lawyerly topics with international intrigue. An attorney named Patrick Lanigan from Biloxi, Mississippi, dies in a car accident. Burned beyond recognition, his body is buried by his grieving widow and business associates. Barely six weeks later, staff at the law offices where he was a partner discover $90 million missing from the firm's coffers. Suspicion immediately focuses on the dead man. Because Patrick was in charge of this particular account, few others could have had access to it.

But the novel doesn't begin with Lanigan's death or with the missing money. Instead readers follow along as a group of thugs, for reasons unknown, pursue a man named Danilo Silva. The thugs nab him in a small town, Ponta Pora, directly west of Sao Paulo, near Brazil's border with Paraguay. A jogger in blue and orange shorts, Silva falls prey to his assailants during his daily run. "On the brink of emaciation," he has spent the past four years living alone in a small house on Rua Tiradentes. When he isn't running, he drives a modest 1983 red Volkswagen Beetle (*Partner* 2).

The men who capture Silva stuff him into the back of a van under boxes of fruit and then drive him past border guards into Paraguay. There he is tied to a plywood rack, drugged, tortured, and then wired to receive progressively stronger electric shocks. Silva's captors, Osmar and Guy, the brutality of their names not a good sign, want to know where the $90 million is.

Gradually, the puzzle pieces begin to fit together. Despite his lean physique, dark hair and skin, square jaw, and slightly pointed nose, Danilo Silva is Patrick Lanigan, down from the 230 pounds he weighed right before the car accident. To become Silva, Lanigan has dyed his hair, run in the sun, and sought the services of a plastic surgeon. Despite the transformation, however, Patrick Lanigan's days on the lam appear to be over. Whoever these thugs are and whoever sent them, they are set on locating the missing fortune and, in the process, probably killing their prey.

Fortunately for Silva/Lanigan, he has a plan in place and a friend and lover to help him. Eva Miranda, a lawyer with the second-largest law firm in Rio de Janiero, has agreed to call the FBI should he suddenly disappear. She has also agreed to take charge of the $90 million Lanigan has deposited in banks in Panama and Bermuda. With Eva Miranda in charge of the money, not even Patrick Lanigan will know where it is. And that's the point. There's no reason to torture or imprison a man who can't access what you are after.

Consistent with Lanigan's plan, the FBI rescues him soon after Eva Miranda calls to report his disappearance. Readers learn that the thugs who have been torturing Patrick Lanigan were hired by Benny Aricia, the man who had possession of the $90 million in the first place. Before that, the money had belonged to a submarine contract firm, actually Aricia himself, "a high official of the offending corporation," who had over-billed the Navy by $600 million (Kisor). "Under the False Claims Act, also known as the Whistle-Blower Law, whoever tips off the government to such fraud may receive 15% of the amount repaid by the offending cor-poration" (Kisor 45). In the case of Benny Aricia, the perpetrator of the fraud profited twice from it. The FBI is interested in the money because, as an arm of the aggrieved government that was defrauded, its job is to locate and reclaim the missing money. In short, everyone wants to bring Lanigan back to the United States to face charges, one of which may now be murder. After all, *someone* was burned up in the wrecked automobile where Patrick Lanigan was supposed to have died.

The rest of the novel traces Lanigan's efforts to get out of his predica-ment: he must satisfy not only the law, but also readers who have come to expect a good-guy hero in a Grisham novel, one like Rudy Baylor or Mitch McDeere. Having left his spouse without so much as a goodbye and having apparently deserted his only child, two-year-old Ashley Nicole, makes Lanigan look evil. Besides, why would an honest attorney following a code of ethics abscond with money not legally his?

In his efforts to get out of trouble, Patrick asks an old friend, Biloxi lawyer Sandy McDermott, to represent him. Few others sympathize with Patrick's situation. Patrick's ex-wife, Trudy, isn't eager to have the husband whose life insurance policy is lavishly supporting her discov-ered to be alive. Although she "still look[s] like everybody's childhood sweetheart," all she wants is for what is Patrick's to be hers (47). Patrick's former colleagues at the firm are more committed to recovering the loot and to keeping "their complicity in a massive defense-contract fraud" unexposed than they are to helping their erstwhile colleague (Dirck 8E). Besides Sandy, Patrick's only supporters are his mother and a judge who hears some of the evidence.

Instead of situating key events in a courtroom, Grisham sets much of the novel in hospitals in Puerto Rico and Biloxi, Mississippi. After his encounter with Osmar and Guy, Patrick needs treatment for the burns he sustained. More to the point from Patrick's perspective, hospitals pro-vide far more competent and hospitable care than does a jail cell. Besides, he easily prefers comfort to correction. From his hospital bed, Patrick can languidly instruct those who are helping him. Gradually, through a series of flashbacks and present events, readers watch him try to extricate himself from the deepest possible mire of suspicion.

CHARACTER DEVELOPMENT

Like most Grisham heroes, Patrick Lanigan is not a fully developed character. Reviewers have described Lanigan's portrayal as "sketchy," "one dimensional," even "cardboard." He was born in New Orleans; he attended law school at Tulane; he lived in Biloxi, Mississippi, before his disappearance; and he has a wife and daughter. After the automobile accident in which he supposedly died, his wife and a business associate unlock his safe deposit box and find the usual things: "the will, two car titles, the deed to the Lanigan home, a life insurance policy in the amount of half a million dollars that Trudy knew about, and another policy for two million that she'd never heard of" (*Partner* 45).

Even Lanigan's transformation into a new and presumably happier self—Danilo Silva—does not prompt Grisham to provide deeper or more complex characterization. Grisham stays resolutely on the outside of his characters, offering up few of Silva's thoughts or feelings. Silva is a jogger. His running course is six miles long. He keeps his few financial records in an apartment in Curitiba. Even in the midst of torture, when Grisham might have depicted a profoundly altered Silva, his narrative brusquely summarizes the action. Electrodes attached to Patrick's, or Danilo's, body by alligator clips lead the character to this speculation: "He thought he counted eight sharp spots on his flesh. Maybe nine" (*Partner* 22).

Readers expecting Lanigan/Silva to be a hero, conventional or otherwise, may be disappointed. Grisham establishes early on that Lanigan has fewer "heroic" qualities than any of his earlier lawyer protagonists. Lanigan is certainly unlike the idealistic Jake Brigance in *A Time to Kill* or the loyal Adam Hall in *The Chamber*.

Even Grisham's more flawed protagonists have some positive qualities. Reggie Love in *The Client*, a recovering alcoholic, has a proverbial heart of gold, at least where preadolescent boys are concerned. Mitch McDeere in *The Firm* is a little greedy, but he couples greed with hard work to get what he wants. Although Mitch crosses a moral line when he is unfaithful to Abby, he never crosses a legal one at Bendini, Lambert & Locke.

Patrick Lanigan, on the other hand, is a total mystery. He steals $90 million from his firm, and readers aren't certain why. Much of the novel's tension grows out of readers trying to figure out whether Lanigan is good or bad. Surely he has some reason for taking the money. We read the novel trying to discover what that reason might be, curious but neither liking nor disliking him as we go.

Heroic or not, there is little, at first, to like about Grisham's protagonist with a double identity. As Patrick Lanigan, he comes across as a hard-driving isolate. It is difficult to imagine him having the imagination and know-how to carry out large-scale theft. As Danilo Silva, he is a boring enigma. A sinewy loner, Danilo Silva lacks any of the charm of a James Bond. He prefers an ascetic's life, having settled nicely into the bland routine of Ponta Pora. How long would Silva have been able to keep the luscious Eva Miranda's interest in such a remote place? Not at all apparently, considering that she stays close to her job in Rio de Janiero, and Silva compensates for her absence by jogging extensively around the far countryside.

Grisham draws Eva Miranda no more fully or sympathetically than he does Patrick Lanigan, focusing on facts about her and not on her feelings. She holds a law degree, with a specialty in trade law, from Catholic University in Rio de Janiero, as well as a degree from Georgetown. Her father lives in Ipanema. She is beautiful, but then women in Grisham's novels seem always to be either unspeakably good-looking or unspeakably bad-looking. As to her motivation for helping Lanigan, she seems to have only one: love. Readers uneasily hope that, like Abby in *The Firm* and like Darby Shaw in *The Pelican Brief*, Miranda will stand happily by her man.

With the novel's two leading characters so flat they need cardboard flaps to hold them erect, it is unsurprising that lesser characters are even flatter. Patrick's wife, Trudy, and her boyfriend, Lance, are greedy and self-absorbed. Lawyers at Patrick Lanigan's old law firm are rotting from within. They are cynical, many of them are alcoholics, and their marriages are on the rocks. In one reviewer's words, "We root for the good guys and boo the bad guys, but our emotional response is muted; it's hard to empathize with cardboard" (Woog M2).

Still, flat but despicable characters can heighten a novel's appeal, given that such characters are easy to hate. Real-world villains generally make us feel ambivalent about them; the extremes of popular fiction provide unambivalent opportunities to like or despise.

PLOT DEVELOPMENT

In AOL's prepublication interview, Grisham pointed out that the plot of *The Partner* has been around for as long as the legal profession. *"The*

Partner is an old story," he said, "Lawyers dream of escaping, preferably with the money. I know several who tried it" (Kornbluth).

Unlike *The Firm*, which Grisham organized chronologically, *The Partner* begins with an engaging in medias res: "They found him in Ponta Pora, a pleasant little town in Brazil, on the border of Paraguay, in a land still known as the frontier" (1). Readers are immediately drawn into the novel's violent introduction, watching as brutal men cause another man to suffer. Following this beginning, Grisham gradually reveals what has led to Danilo Silva's capture and torture. These events, of course, take place back in the United States and involve Silva's original identity as Patrick Lanigan.

In *The Partner*, Grisham uses a tried-and-true method of organizing chapters. As he has done in all his novels, he breaks each of *The Partner*'s chapters, 43 in all, into several short episodes, each advancing the action and increasing suspense. In *The Partner*, however, episodes do not contain material as disparate as the material in novels such as *The Client* in which Grisham develops four related plot lines and alternates among them within single chapters. Episodes in *The Partner* often just mark a pause in a single narrative strand.

The Partner is unlike most Grisham novels in that it does not address a hot legal or social issue: at issue in other novels were insurance scams in *The Rainmaker*, the death penalty in *The Chamber*, and tobacco litigation in *The Runaway Jury*. The closest *The Partner* comes to an issue-driven plot is Lanigan's midlife disenchantment with materialism in the United States, and even that issue is hard to take seriously given that one focus of the novel is Lanigan's effort to steal $90 million dollars.

Otherwise, *The Partner* keeps readers engaged by implicitly posing questions that it postpones answering (Is Patrick to be liked or despised? Will he get away with whatever crimes he has committed? Why would an apparently responsible man run out on his own child?) and by putting Patrick into what appears to be a "no win" situation. There seems to be no way he could be totally innocent of the crimes he has supposedly committed.

Without a social issue driving it, *The Partner* has no place for a traditional hero who captures the bad guys and cleans up the town. The price, of course, is that the novel lacks "do-gooder passion" (Singer 33). Readers do not respond to the novel with moral or ethical urgency. They are more likely to read only to find out what happens in the end.

As he does in his other novels, Grisham uses a shifting narrative perspective in *The Partner*. Although he never explores the psyches of individual narrators, he tells the story from differing characters' points of view. In chapter 1, for instance, he reports events first from Guy's and Osmar's points of view and then from Danilo's perspective, from Osmar's alone, from Eva Miranda's, and, finally, from Guy's once again.

Small plot errors and implausibilities suggest the book may have been rushed to press. One reviewer wondered why Patrick, an apparent expert in electronic surveillance, would talk so freely in his hospital room, especially considering that it would very likely have been bugged (Holt E3). When Grisham resolves issues, he sometimes does so brusquely and without properly preparing his readers. For example, in a denouement, Grisham explains that Lanigan abandons Ashley Nicole, but not until he has secured a DNA test that proves their genes don't match. According to one reviewer, "Only a lawyer would maintain that a parent would stop loving a child he had been fondly raising . . . because he found out it wasn't biologically his" (Amidon).

Reviewers, even those with little else to like, have praised *The Partner*'s plot. A reviewer for the *Seattle Times* noted that it is "a prime example of what its author does very well—the best example, I think, since *The Firm*, the book that made him famous." Grisham comes up with "a single, foolproof, cast-iron idea that taps into the public imagination—and run[s] with it" (Woog M2).

The few reviewers who have criticized the plot feel that Grisham uses in the novel too many devices from his earlier books: international money wires, a beautiful woman assisting a virile hero, the junior lawyer trying to outwit his more senior partners. At least one reviewer, a writer for the *Chicago Sun-Times*, thought the plot was "manipulative," with Grisham withholding information from readers that characters in the novel already know (Kisor 45).

Readers disappointed by *The Partner*'s surprise ending should consult with Ron Berthel of the Associated Press, who claims that Grisham issued warnings of what was to come. According to Bethel, only readers "who did not pick up on the two big clues Grisham leaves" will be shocked by the novel's end (Pate F12). He has never identified, however, what those "two big clues" are.

SOCIAL AND LITERARY CONTEXTS

The writing of Grisham's eighth novel affirms at least one American Dream. A hardworking young novelist, John Grisham, originally of modest means, travels to Ponta Pora, Brazil, in 1993, with a group from his church. The group is there to build a small chapel as well as to supply a remote area with medical care and, Grisham says, "a ton of pharmaceuticals" (Kelly 7D). But the enterprising writer, who drives around town picking up building supplies because, as he says, he is too inept to so much as drive a nail, accomplishes more than the construction of worship space. He dreams up his eighth novel, which will make him still richer than he already is.

This affirmation of the American bootstraps myth couples with an intriguing note from mid-twentieth-century history. While chatting with the locals, the writer hears about "a little cafe there, in town, where every day these old guys with gray hair would meet and have lunch. Sausage and beer. And all you could hear being spoken was German." Grisham continues, "They were old Nazis. . . . I thought, 'It would be a very easy place to hide if you were on the run'" (Kelly 7D). From that small beginning, Grisham imagines who else might hide in Ponta Pora and what a life on the run might be like. Philanthropy and history collide.

THEMATIC ISSUES

The theme of "dropping out" dominates in *The Partner*. Grisham assumes that his audience will be at least partially sympathetic to Patrick Lanigan, who chooses life in a sleepy Brazilian town over a dreary law career in Biloxi.

But it's not just any rat race that Patrick drops out of. As Grisham describes it, the race is a decidedly American one. The America that Lanigan rejects is greedy, materialistic, and spiritually bankrupt. It is, as one reviewer puts it, "a gigantic fraud." Although Ponta Pora "may be just as corrupt as the United States . . . it doesn't pretend to be anything more. Its air may be as polluted as ours, but not with hypocrisy. There will be no national fairy tales of innocence and good intentions, and no comforting bedtime stories like the Declaration of Independence or the Gettysburg Address" (Marcus E2).

America's materialistic culture, as Grisham constructs it, has a strong female as well as male component. Trudy, Patrick's wife, embodies all of the worst qualities of American life. She selfishly seeks her own pleasures without regard for anyone else. Patrick's male law partners are equally self-absorbed. All they want is more, regardless of whether they get it legally or illegally. Trudy's boyfriend, Lance, a small-time drug runner and an apparent stud in bed, completes the ugly picture. Of course, Patrick himself is also the embodiment of materialism because the underlying point of his escape from the United States is personal gain.

In creating a character who escapes from everyday social pressures, Grisham joins many writers of the traditional American novel who deal with the same issue. Patrick Lanigan shares much in common with Ahab and Ishmael in *Moby Dick*, Huck and Jim in *Huckleberry Finn*, and Rip Van Winkle in the Washington Irving tale by that name. Like these classic American heroes, Patrick Lanigan, for good or ill, joyously chucks everything and sets "out for the Territory ahead" (Twain 368).

Even though he is churning out a legal thriller and not a work of so-called serious literature, Grisham seems to have explicitly created in Patrick Lanigan an archetypal American hero. At one point, Grisham's Patrick self-consciously says, "Life's always better on the beach or in the mountains. Problems can be left behind. It's inbred in us. We're the products of immigrants who left miserable conditions and came here in search of a better life. And they kept moving west, packing up and leaving, always looking for the pot of gold. Now, there's no place to go" (394–95). Such cultural and historical awareness on Patrick's part may surprise some readers since Patrick doesn't go in much for self-reflection.

In fact, Dale Singer called Grisham's philosophizing a "mismatch" with the rest of the novel, noting that "its wistfulness adds another false note" (33). Although Patrick's speech seems out of place given *The Partner*'s context and style, Grisham was undoubtedly aware of what he was doing and liked the idea. Still, Grisham should have done more to develop his point. He has Patrick assign cultural significance to his own behavior and then drops the discussion.

Although a *Boston Globe* reviewer called *The Partner*'s theme of dropping out "almost universal," it probably has more male than female appeal (Dyer C6). How often does one hear some version of a woman leaving behind her husband and children, having faked her death in a car accident or having left a note for the distraught husband to find? In fact, American women are more likely to be in Trudy's situation, with a husband who ducks out of town, leaving them behind to raise the children and, as Trudy does so well, start a new life. But this does not account for the phenomenal success of Grisham's novel among female readers. Do they see their lives reflected in Patrick Lanigan's, and if so, how do they avoid seeing that their predicaments may be more like Trudy's than his?

The novel also deals with the emotional pangs of midlife. Before leaving Biloxi behind, Patrick measures his bleak life against a fantasy existence elsewhere. Of course, life in the here and now comes up wanting. The presence of lack and loss as a theme may help account for the novel's success on planes and in airport lounges. Middle-aged, middle-class readers, male and female alike, numbly flying from Los Angeles to New York or from New Orleans to Chicago are likely to see in *The Partner* a character who dares to act, albeit in a grandiose and illegal way, when he realizes his life lacks verve and meaning.

The novel's title leads to a final, if ironic, theme. Presumably, a novel titled *The Partner* would concern characters' connectedness to each other. In Grisham's telling of Patrick Lanigan's story, that is not the case. Lanigan is everyone's and no one's partner at the same time. Although he has been a partner in a law firm, a partner to a wife, and a partner with Eva Miranda in eluding apprehension, no character could embody "partner-lessness" better than Lanigan does. In fact, he double-crosses or betrays his "partner" in two of those three relationships.

The book's central question is whether the third key player, Eva Miranda, will be a good or bad partner to Patrick. To protect himself and his money, Lanigan has no choice but to involve Miranda in his gigantic scheme. In doing so, however, he must trust her with the $90 million he has stolen. The novel shows whether Lanigan's faith in Eva is wisely placed and presents the reader with the larger question of whether any of us can fully trust those we have chosen to love.

REVIEWS OF THE NOVEL

Reviewers of *The Partner* generally have applauded it. Even those who may not care for Grisham's novel have been savvy enough not to criticize it too harshly, given that every book Grisham writes seems to zoom to bestseller status and, in the process, earn its author another few million dollars.

Still, some of the novel's reviewers have been noncommittal. A *Publishers Weekly* reviewer, for example, wrote only that *The Partner* is about a world where "money rules" (Maryles 18). In making this observation, the reviewer showed more interest in the path by which the novel traveled to top-seller stardom than in whether it belongs there in the first place. It's hard to tell whether the *Kansas City Star* reviewer was being respectful or snide when she called Grisham "the master of in-flight entertainment" (Pate E7).

Clearly positive about the novel, the *Atlanta Constitution* called it "a super read and a super seller" (Warmbold 1D). The *Denver Post* labeled it a "great yarn" (Giffin E12), and a reviewer for the *Christian Science Monitor* agreed that "all the convoluted elements of a page-turning thriller are here: the hard edge of a Raymond Chandler; the brilliant legal maneuvering of an Erle Stanley Gardner; the surprise ending of an O. Henry or an Agatha Christie" (Goodrich 13).

Writing for the _San Francisco Chronicle,_ Patricia Holt was less benign. Labeling _The Partner_ Grisham's "oddest novel," she wondered "how many readers will feel cheated by a story that takes 100 pages to get our attention, another hundred to weave a not-so-magical spell and the last 150 or so creating a cardboard hero" (E3). _USA Today_'s reviewer suggested that Grisham take a break from "cranking out book after book" in order to avoid "rehashing variations on the same plot" (Donahue 1D).

Everyday readers reporting online have been almost unanimously thrilled with Grisham's eighth novel, especially its action and suspense. Still, some have expressed frustration with its ending. One reader from Texas wrote that the conclusion "might make you want to hurl the book against the wall." And a reader from Pennsylvania offered a more measured response: "I truly hope [Grisham] decides to write a sequel to explain the maddening ending."

3

The Street Lawyer
(1998)

On February 4, 1998, Doubleday released *The Street Lawyer*, John Grisham's "shortest novel to date" at 350 pages, confidently dropping "2.8 million copies [at $27.95] on bookstores across the country" (Baldacci). In this, his ninth novel, Grisham returned to social issues and the law. Earlier books had dealt with race relations, capital punishment, insurance fraud, and Big Tobacco. Now came *The Street Lawyer*, about poverty and homelessness and focusing as well on big cities' inadequate responses, legal and otherwise, to these two related problems.

It's easy to see why Grisham's publishers would print so many copies of his latest thriller and be confident they would reach a large reading audience. In the seven years between publication of *The Firm* in 1991 and *The Street Lawyer* in 1998, celebrity trials in the United States had become "a national obsession" (Kakutani). Americans had been riveted by cases involving O. J. Simpson, the Menendez brothers, and Whitewater, as well as legal matters surrounding Bill Clinton's White House sex scandal. Besides an entire television channel devoted to court cases, CNN's *Burden of Proof* had made viewers "familiar with legal lingo" (Kakutani). Additionally, the nationally syndicated *Judge Judy* had become a popular and important show on ABC, and other networks offered similar fare.

But other cultural factors ensured Grisham a large reading audience for *The Street Lawyer* as well, among them "the globalization of American culture[,] the efflorescence of the superstore and its showcasing of brand-name books, and Hollywood's insatiable appetite for formulaic thrillers" (Kakutani). In fact, Grisham's books have been among those singled out for promotion through publication parties at giant chain bookstores.

THE PLOT

As often happens in a John Grisham novel, the action in *The Street Lawyer* begins abruptly. After sharing an elevator to the sixth floor of his office building with a homeless man, Michael Brock, an up-and-coming attorney in the Washington, D.C., firm of Drake & Sweeney, stares aghast as the man shoots up his firm's sixth-floor reception area and then takes Michael and seven of the firm's lawyers hostage. In a conference room off reception, the man instructs Michael to tie his colleagues' hands. To convince everyone that he means business, the man peels off several layers of clothes to reveal a belt of dynamite strapped to his waist.

He demands the possessions his hostages are carrying in their pockets, and quickly, watches, wallets, and coins from many pockets are tossed together into a single black briefcase. The man then forces Michael to ask a managing partner via speakerphone for everyone's tax returns from the previous year. Fifteen minutes later, this demand is met.

With everyone's tax returns in hand, the man—Grisham at first calls him Mister—harangues his hostages, demanding to know why they've given so little to charity. He tells Michael to list everyone in the room by name, to record that person's salary next to his name, and to note in a third column how much each has donated to charitable causes. The man asks for nothing but information and makes no verbal threats. Instead he holds a red wire presumably attached to the dynamite pack at his waist. When the group's paltry contributions are made public, Mister forces each hostage to further distinguish between his contributions to rich people's charities—such as the symphony—and real charity: feeding the poor. He asks three questions: How much to clinics? Soup kitchens? Homeless shelters? The charitable records of those assembled look even worse than they did before.

Eventually, Mister orders food for the group from a nearby free kitchen. When the soup and bread arrive, a cart carrying this poor-people provender for the lawyers to share is to be wheeled into the conference room. But a sniper is lurking behind a desk in the reception area. When the door opens and someone bends down to pull in the food cart, the sniper gets his shot off. It blows away Mister's head. Everyone is safe, except for Michael Brock. Although he isn't physically injured, he is emotionally wrecked. At one point, he looks at his fellow hostages, sees them from the perspective of Mister, and acknowledges to himself that they are "greedy bastards" (20).

Rescuers immediately whisk Michael to a small gym in the basement of the building, only to find that the blood coating his body is Mister's, not his. Michael looks around for his wife because the families of all the other hostages have gathered. But Claire is not there. Claire is not at home either, and Michael is reminded of how much his career has damaged his marriage. The pattern is similar to that of other Grisham heroes. Michael graduates from Yale Law School and joins a prestigious Washington law firm. Although he meets his future wife soon after arriving in D.C., he doesn't insist on balancing personal and professional, and instead he works hours that are stolen, he now realizes, from his marriage. To fill her empty life, it seems, his wife decides to go to medical school.

Awakening the morning after the tragedy, Michael still feels traumatized. The papers contain information about Mister. He was DeVon Hardy, a 45-year-old Vietnam veteran with a record of burglary and drug abuse. He was homeless, having recently been evicted from the warehouse where he'd been living. Did attorneys from Michael's firm handle the eviction, Michael wonders? It is something they apparently often do. Michael reads in the newspapers that the dynamite strapped to DeVon's waist wasn't dynamite at all. DeVon had cut up a broom handle, wrapped pieces of it in tape, and slung them around himself in such a way as to make Michael and his associates believe they were explosives.

Although Michael could take a few days off to recover from what has happened to him, he goes to work, arriving at the office to find the previous day's bloody conference room fully restored. The mess has been scrubbed away and painted over, a pricey new Oriental rug already replacing the old gore-spattered one. Suddenly, Michael can't stand to stay where he is. He leaves the office, thinking that his colleagues "would just have to give me a break" (37).

Much of the information about DeVon Hardy in the papers has been provided by Mordecai Green, director of the 14th Street Legal Clinic. Michael drives to the clinic to meet Mordecai, and from him, he learns more about DeVon, in particular that DeVon and the other tenants at the warehouse probably didn't receive notice before being evicted, even though they were paying rent.

Not sure why he is doing so, Michael accepts Mordecai's invitation to volunteer at a soup kitchen, where he will make bologna and peanut butter sandwiches. During his first night on the job, he befriends Ontario, a little boy staying at the shelter with his mother and siblings.

Michael learns at the soup kitchen that money supporting the 14th Street Legal Clinic is in short supply. Mordecai's law office operates on funds provided by something called the Cohen Trust. Unfortunately, others have mismanaged the trust, and each year, the firm receives less and less money. Eventually, Mordecai says, the source will dry up, and unless some other funding comes along, the clinic will be out of business.

Ontario and his family do not show up at the shelter the next day, and soon, television newscasts are reporting the deaths of a woman and children in a car near Fort Totten Park in the northeast part of the city. Evicted from their home and living in the family car, they asphyxiated from breathing exhaust fumes. The dead woman's name is Lontae Burton; the dead children are Temeko, Alonzo, Dante, and little Ontario, age four. This is the second time in a week that Michael has encountered death close at hand. "I cursed Mister for derailing my life. I cursed Mordecai for making me feel guilty. And Ontario for breaking my heart" (86).

Soon Mordecai offers Michael full partnership in the law clinic, something that Drake & Sweeney has yet to do. Making Michael's decision easier, an envelope mysteriously appears on his desk at Drake & Sweeney. In it is incontrovertible evidence that the firm not only mishandled the eviction of DeVon Hardy, but also is responsible for evicting Lontae Burton and her children from a place called RiverOaks. In response, Michael resigns from Drake & Sweeney.

Returning to his old office one more time, Michael discovers that someone has deposited another file on his desk. This one contains two keys—one to a colleague's office door and one to a file cabinet in that same office. Eventually using the keys, Michael takes a file marked RiverOaks/TAG, Inc., which contains even more proof of Drake & Sweeney's illegal actions. Just after escaping the office with the file, Michael is involved in an automobile accident when a drug bust goes awry, and a Jaguar collides with his Lexus, a vestige of his former life. Michael awakens in the hospital, suddenly aware that the file he has stolen is still in his wrecked car, wherever it might be. Mordecai eventually finds Michael's car at a police impoundment lot, and Michael retrieves the file.

Michael is working in his new office over the weekend when an old friend from Drake & Sweeney stops by. Michael confesses to having the file, adding that information in it will make Drake & Sweeney look bad if he takes it public. The friend tries to negotiate peace, but Michael says, "It's too late. People are dead" (143).

With Mordecai's support, Michael continues to collect evidence about Drake & Sweeney's involvement in the evictions of DeVon Hardy and Lontae Burton. To that end, they visit a soup kitchen, where they locate another person who was evicted along with Hardy and Burton. This young man confirms what Mordecai and Michael strongly suspect: the people evicted at RiverOaks were indeed rent-paying tenants who deserved legal protection. They did not get that protection, and, furthermore, Drake & Sweeney was deeply involved in their illegal evictions. Michael realizes that because the evictions resulted in the deaths of several tenants, including Michael's young friend Ontario, Drake & Sweeney is even more vulnerable to prosecution. Armed with this information, Michael underestimates the lengths Drake & Sweeney will go to get its missing file back. He is in his office working on a client's food stamps when a police officer arrives to arrest him. Before Mordecai can bail him out of jail, thugs have taken Michael's shoes and jacket and beaten him.

After gathering still more evidence against Drake & Sweeney, Michael and Mordecai prepare to file a lawsuit in Lontae's name. Shortly thereafter, Mordecai enters settlement negotiations on Michael's behalf with Drake & Sweeney. The eventual settlements are a compromise. As for Lontae's suit, Michael and Mordecai get the $5 million they have sued for, but Drake & Sweeney and the other litigants are allowed to pay over time. In terms of a settlement between Michael and Drake & Sweeney, Michael's law license is suspended for nine months for the file theft, but he is not disbarred or suspended for the amount of time requested by Drake & Sweeney. The 14th Street Legal Clinic's short-term take is $500,000. Another $500,000 goes to refresh the trust that has been supporting them: victory at last.

CHARACTER DEVELOPMENT

Like most reviews of Grisham's work, those concerning *The Street Lawyer* say character development is the novel's greatest weakness. Such a weakness in this particular work is especially unfortunate because the book's effect depends largely on readers believing in and empathizing with Michael Brock in his conversion from high-paid, high-powered junior attorney to underpaid street lawyer.

And they can't, really. As a *New York Times* reviewer notes, "Mr. Grisham gives us no insight into Michael's emotional makeup, because he defines him purely through externals—what he wears, what he drives, what he earns" (Kakutani). Although at least one critic defends him—labeling him Mitch McDeere but with "a much larger conscience" (Ogle)—it is apparent there is "no subtlety or nuance to Michael's story" (Kakutani).

In fact, probably because Michael does not seem real, he is not particularly likeable either, even after his conversion. In fact, "Michael emerges as a particularly unsympathetic hero: sanctimonious, self-dramatizing and willfully adolescent . . . who speaks almost entirely in clichés: he talks about being 'back at full throttle' and being his 'usual hard-charging self.' To a friend he says he's 'found a calling'; to his brother, he says 'I've lost my love for money. It's the curse of the devil'" (Kakutani).

Most problematic is Michael's quick transformation from conscientious legal drudge to socially committed attorney. It is hard to imagine someone who has spent a lifetime preparing to be a corporate lawyer and in fact reaching that goal suddenly making Michael's extraordinary about-face. Said the *Miami Herald*, "Mike's transformation happens with the speed of light. You open the book, he's a corporate lawyer. Mere pages later, he's ready to quit" (Ogle). Describing the "inner turmoil" leading to Michael's change of heart "is not Grisham's strength ('My soul kept me awake,' Michael confesses)" (Ogle). Even Rene Heybach of the *Chicago Sun-Times*, who liked the book, admitted that Michael's "metamorphosis . . . is less than fully explored by Grisham" (4).

Even assuming Michael could make such a drastic change in his life, a man of his character and training would be unlikely to harangue others about the correctness of his actions. Reviewers have pointed out this discrepancy, saying they resent Michael's sanctimonious proselytizing. One such reviewer noted that "Michael's one-month transformation from yuppie creep to socially conscious 'street lawyer' hardly qualifies him to deliver homilies about the homeless—not that that stops him" (Baldacci).

Furthermore, readers expect secondary characters to be flat, but not as flat as those in *The Street Lawyer*. Not only do they tend to be one-dimensional, but they also resemble the kind of stereotypes often portrayed in film. It's as if Grisham was writing with the goal of selling his novel to Hollywood. There are

> parts for a grandstanding black lawyer (Morgan Freeman), a Calvin Klein glasses-type pretty boy (Matthew McConaughey) and a senior actor who can do lofty authority, plus change of heart (Gene Hackman), as well as major opportunities for general impoverished suffering and for dozens of Hollywood film vehicles to descend on gritty Washington locations (soup

kitchens and squats). The only big difference is the absence of a Christmas setting and calling it *A Christmas Carol.* (Petit)

When a television project based on the novel did get underway, the cast wasn't quite as distinguished (or, at least, as expensive) as the one fantasized by Petit. Hal Holbrook was the "senior actor" able to do "lofty authority"; Eddie Cibrian took the Matthew McConaughey part. At last report, a pilot had aired, but the series project had been dropped from development.

Still, among secondary characters, one stands out. Although something of a cliché, Mordecai Green is among the novel's more interesting characters, a black man representative of those working within the legal system in Washington, D.C., to help the poor. Grisham evidently came into contact with people like Mordecai, and perhaps the actual "Mordecai," while doing research for his book. In an author's note, he thanks "the real Mordecai Greens, [and pays] quiet tribute [to their] work in the trenches" (312).

PLOT DEVELOPMENT

One of Grisham's strengths as a writer is his ability to draw readers quickly into the action. This is particularly true of *The Street Lawyer*'s opening scene. Grisham's strategy of having a homeless man with moxie hold an office full of attorneys hostage gives the novel a powerful start. The bloody aftermath of the homeless man's actions is sure to hold readers' attention well into the body of the novel. One reviewer even called the *Street Lawyer*'s introduction "the best scene Grisham has ever put on paper" (Sutherland).

The Street Lawyer is in some ways a retelling of Charles Dickens's *A Christmas Carol* minus really cold weather and Tiny Tim. At the start of the novel, Michael Brock is as rigid and self-consciously tight-fisted as Ebenezer Scrooge. During the ensuing four weeks, he learns to empathize with the poor. That said, Dickens's Scrooge has to work harder than Michael Brock does to achieve transformation. He must revisit a lifetime of scenes detailing his own selfishness, and he must have a supernatural escort with him at all times. Not so for Michael Brock. One half hour of being held hostage by the homeless DeVon Hardy is apparently enough to change Michael's values forever.

Grisham uses "a familiar Grisham recipe" in structuring *The Street Lawyer* (Kakutani). As in each of his earlier novels, Grisham juxtaposes several disconnected storylines within 39 short—usually 10-page—chapters. That technique has proven to work well for him, enabling readers to whisk through a Grisham novel, connect the various stories within chapters, make meaning, and hunger for more.

The plot line of *The Street Lawyer* should be familiar to anyone who has already read Grisham. *The Street Lawyer* pits "an honest lawyer— usually a southerner about Grisham's age—against a corrupt 'system'" (Sutherland). In the course of earlier novels, the corrupt system has been the mafia, the FBI, big business, and the Ku Klux Klan. "Interestingly, in *The Street Lawyer* the evil system the lawyer takes on is the law itself" (Sutherland). Of course, there are other "corrupt systems" in (or notice- ably absent from) the novel, among them the welfare system, children's services, and the "silk-stocking" law firms focused on billable hours (*Street Lawyer* 35).

Grisham does a good job overall of handling plot. One reviewer wrote that the novel includes a few well-devised surprises (Sutherland). Another praised Grisham's dialogue, calling it "taut" (Baldacci). Like Grisham's other novels, this one propels readers forward through the story. Like the novel or not, people generally keep reading.

Not everyone, however, is satisfied by *The Street Lawyer*'s storyline, and it is true that Grisham's research for the novel occasionally feels intrusive. Here, for example, is Michael describing the Community for Creative Nonviolence.

> The CCNV was founded in the early seventies by a group of war protestors who had assembled in Washington to torment the government. They lived together in a house in Northwest. During their protests around the Capitol, they met homeless veterans of Vietnam, and began taking them in. They moved to larger quarters, various places around the city, and their numbers grew. After the war, they turned their attention to the plight of the D.C. homeless. In the early eighties, an activ- ist named Mitch Snyder appeared on the scene, and quickly became a passionate and noisy voice for street people. (165)

There is more to this passage. It continues for a full page, interrupting Michael Brock's first-person narrative. Sections of the novel such as this one may be what caused one reviewer to complain that Grisham lets "gobbets of research clog his story" (Dyer), another to say the plot has "no twists or turns . . . just a litany of breast-beating, tear-jerking pathos on behalf of poor people" (Millar), and a third to claim the novel is "curiously lacking in action" (Ogle).

Perhaps the most frequently voiced complaint about plot has to do with plausibility. The complaint seems well founded: "Mr. Grisham would have us believe that Mister's jeremiad about homelessness has induced a sudden change of heart in Michael, that it has made him want to abandon the fast track corporate life and go into public-interest law" (Kakutani). The novel simply doesn't adequately support this shift in thinking. A more likely scenario would have Michael profoundly resenting the man who had so badly frightened him and turning his back on others like DeVon.

SOCIAL CONTEXTS

Even though his handling of research on *The Street Lawyer* sometimes feels a bit heavy-handed, Grisham works hard to provide readers with social and historical context for his discussion of homelessness and poverty in Washington, D.C. Rightly, he points out how ironic it is that the capital of the richest nation on earth should be home to so many destitute people. Whatever criticisms have been leveled at the novel, Grisham is to be admired for taking on an issue about which he apparently feels strongly.

Reviewer Rene Heybach, writing in the *Chicago Sun-Times,* loudly applauded Grisham's efforts on behalf of the destitute. A "street lawyer" herself, she wrote that she appreciates the way Grisham glamorized her work, "adding a certain sense of action, even danger, to our typical notion of an attorney," and that she hopes the book will provide "a new angle for funding." The problem, she noted, is that "legal services for the poor have been the focus of a prolonged attack by Congress. Its budget—a thirty percent reduction in the past three years [as of 1998]—is now too meager to serve more than a fraction of our nation's impoverished and has forced poor people's lawyers to seek alternative funding to provide the legal representation that rich people expect" (Heybach).

Besides casting street lawyers in a positive light, the novel accurately portrays the work these professionals do. As Heybach attests, it cannot be easy coming "into contact every day with people who . . . face life on the street, trying to survive cold, hunger, and violence." Here is a book that "grabs us by the collar . . . and dares us to ignore the lessons homeless people can teach America—when we are forced to listen" (Holt).

But the situation is a complex one, with no single right answer and no pure heroes or villains. Patricia Holt's review for the *San Francisco Chronicle* reminds us, "We come to respect the paradox faced by anyone who works with the homeless. Because of their indomitable spirit in surviving each exhausting and calamitous day, the homeless easily win our admiration; yet their nomadic natures, hopeless addictions and tendency to abandon loved ones can just as easily break the hearts of those who care" (E1).

THEMATIC ISSUES

The Street Lawyer doesn't do a "Dostoevski-like exploration of truth or conflict. It is just an entertaining read with an important theme" (Heybach). It asks readers to consider the question of responsibility. To what extent must U.S. citizens help the poor among us, and how far should we go to provide that assistance? It reminds us that we are responsible for one another and that we forget that lesson at our own and our country's peril. In connection with that theme, Rene Heybach challenges "those who toil at 'Drake & Sweeneys' to cross the line. Wealth and power mean nothing if you cannot recognize the humanity in a man you pass on the street" (show 4).

A second theme is that many of the poor have little or no choice in the matter of their own poverty, a message our bootstraps culture sometimes prefers to ignore. Mordecai Green states the case: "Everybody has to be somewhere. These people have no alternatives. If you're hungry, you beg for food. If you're tired, then you sleep wherever you can find a spot. If you're homeless, you have to live somewhere" (147). According to Patricia Holt, "the message could be preachy and tiresome, but Grisham's gift of weaving in hot legal cases with urgent confrontations and personal catastrophes saves it" (E1).

Others disagree with Holt about the subtlety of *The Street Lawyer*'s message, noting that Grisham "has developed the same disease that ails film director Oliver Stone. He wields his theme like a club and clobbers you senseless until you're too bleary-eyed to see the story" (Ogle). As one critic wrote, "There has always been a streak of piety in Grisham's fiction. In *The Street Lawyer* it is so broad that his modest narrative technique creaks under the weight of sermonizing. One finishes the book longing for a good (i.e. malicious) lawyer joke" (Sutherland).

A third theme of the novel has to do with how best to live life. The most obvious answer Grisham gives is to do good things. In the process, though, he says to expect, and even welcome, change. The events of *The Street Lawyer* take place over 32 days. During that time, Michael Brock's life undergoes a transformation. Everything in the present shifts, as do his future prospects. The novel ends with Michael reflecting on what has happened: "Thirty-two days earlier I had been married to someone else, living in a different apartment, working in a different firm, a complete stranger to the woman I was now holding. How could life change so drastically in a month?" (309). And yet it has, and for the better, it seems. Now he works for love, not money, and along the way, he has found a partner whose priorities are similar to his.

REVIEWS OF THE NOVEL

Reviews of *The Street Lawyer* tend to be mostly negative, but they cover the gamut: good, bad, and in between. Positive appraisals generally argue the novel performs an important social function by letting readers know about the problems of homeless people. Not surprisingly, attorney-reviewer Rene Heybach, a strong supporter of the novel, likes it because it affirms that "transformation is possible and . . . representing the poorest people in our city [Washington, D.C.] is absolutely the best thing a person with a law degree can do." Another reviewer who likes *The Street Lawyer* wrote that it "shows not only that [Grisham] has his finger on the public pulse but that he's also out to prick its conscience. Using his proven David vs. Goliath formula, he's written his most crusading and appealing story since 1995's *The Rainmaker*" (Pate).

Some reviewers sit on the fence, one noting that *The Street Lawyer* is "one of Grisham's thinner books, episodic and one dimensional, sorely lacking in complexity and fully developed characters. . . . Still the plot surges forward, pulling us along as we turn those pages a mile a minute" (Holt). Another reviewer has pointed out the usual disparity between reviewers' judgments and popular reactions to Grisham's books, concluding that this one "is certainly not art, and not even respectable pop culture; equally certainly, it will turn the attention of millions of readers—and, in time, even moviegoers—to a subject they'd rather walk past" (Dyer).

The remarks of those who don't care for *The Street Lawyer* range from polite to snide. One such reviewer gently noted, "There was a depth and thoughtfulness to earlier novels . . . that seems lacking in *The Street Lawyer*" (Donahue). Another wrote that "Grisham, trying for a sympathetic, socially relevant subplot, got stuck in the same trap most of us face when homelessness greets us on the street: We do not want to get too close" (Baldacci).

Less generous reactions have included the following: "As thrillers go, this one is a pot-boiler that never starts to simmer" (Millar); "It is not easy to see why Grisham is a bestseller. He doesn't write well, his plots are repetitive and unimaginative (compared, say, to Scott Turow), and he publishes too much" (Sutherland). Describing the novel as "stilted" and "jerry-built," another critic judged *The Street Lawyer* to be "a perfunctory name brand novel with an unlikable hero, a slapdash plot and some truly awful prose" (Kakutani). One reviewer focused less on the novel and more on his obligations as a critic: "Even with dull writers," he wrote, "one makes an effort to write an entertaining review—out of vanity, and for the reader—but with Grisham can one be bothered?" (Petit).

4

The Testament
(1999)

The Testament was a victory for John Grisham, whose previous novel, *The Street Lawyer*, sold very well, but was roundly criticized in newspapers across the United States. As one reviewer noted after reading *The Testament*, "Grisham appears fully recovered from the by-the-number routine that made *The Street Lawyer* . . . a stern test of fan loyalty" (Bell). In *The Testament*, his tenth novel, Grisham becomes downright experimental, playing games with point of view, stretching well-established plot patterns, introducing issues of faith and identity, and exceeding the boundaries of legal thriller conventions.

If Grisham's publishers were made nervous by *The Street Lawyer*'s critical reception, they didn't show it in their prepublication fanfare for *The Testament*. As with Grisham's two previous novels, Doubleday released a first printing of 2.8 million copies, soon followed by a second printing of 100,000 ("Twentieth-Century American Bestsellers"). Even before the novel's release date, Doubleday had e-mailed its second and third chapters to Grisham fans registered at the writer's official Web site. Partnering this time with MSNBC and Hewlett Packard, Doubleday also did a Web promotion for the novel that included trivia and novel excerpts. As a further marketing strategy, Doubleday's owner, Random House, linked up with John Grisham's Web site. These efforts evidently paid off. In its first year, *The Testament* sold an astounding 2,475,000 hardcover copies, and publishers of the paperback version, Dell's Island, sold 3,875,000 paperback copies (Bestsellers).

THE PLOT

On Monday, December 9, 1996, Troy Phelan, a billionaire many times over, claims to be reapportioning his money via a new will. His family members—including three ex-wives—have gathered at Troy's request to witness the event. Everyone will be in the same building when Troy signs the will, but family will not be physically present at the signing. Instead they will be downstairs watching via closed-circuit television while Phelan conducts business from his top-floor office suite.

Phelan hates his ex-wives, Lillian, Janie, and Tira. He also hates his children. He even hates his servant, Snead, who takes care of his many needs. Everyone knows Troy Phelan will soon die. He is an old, sick man and cruel and ugly to the bone.

When the ceremony begins—and Phelan makes sure the signing is a ceremony—he first proves to a panel of psychiatrists brought in for the occasion that he is of sound enough mind to sign a will. Phelan has circulated rumors that the latest will awards most of his money to his children and grandchildren. But what he puts his signature to, no one ever sees. He signs the first will, but holds on to it while his assorted family groupings are escorted from the building. Then, still on camera but without any family present, he pulls an envelope out of his robe and signs a completely new will that revokes all others. Having done so, he stands up from his wheelchair—amazing to the psychologists and his lawyer who assumed he couldn't walk—and hurls himself off of a narrow rooftop terrace to the ground below.

With Troy Phelan dead and no longer able to serve as narrator, several third-person voices begin relating events at the start of chapter 3. Partway through, Josh Stafford, Troy Phelan's attorney, takes over, reading Phelan's instructions and the new will aloud on camera. Phelan has left all his money to an illegitimate daughter whom no one has ever heard of: Rachel Lane, a World Tribes missionary in the Brazilian borderlands near Bolivia.

But at first, the family doesn't know about the new will. According to instructions Phelan left to Josh, the will's contents must not be made public for a month after his death, long after Phelan's ashes have been scattered over land he owned in Wyoming. Rejoicing at the wealth soon to be theirs, the survivors begin profligate spending. TJ (Troy Jr.) buys two new Porsches. A grandson purchases a huge supply of dope.

Meanwhile, Josh Stafford and his partners begin the search for Rachel Lane. Before his death, Phelan pinpointed her location, give or take a few tens of thousands of acres, but the approximate knowledge is not enough under these new circumstances. The heiress—now one of the world's richest—must be found, the fortune officially handed over.

To find Rachel, Phelan's legal team selects a recovering alcoholic associate, Nate O'Riley. At one time a litigator with a superb reputation, O'Riley has spent the past several months in an alcohol and drug rehabilitation center, and now he is about to be released. Josh offers Nate a thousand dollars a day plus expenses to find Rachel, and Nate agrees to make the trip to Brazil's largest backwater. From this point on, the novel veers back and forth between Brazil, where Nate is pursuing Rachel, and the Washington, D.C., area where Troy Phelan's lawyers and family are.

Three flights bring Nate to Brazil's Corumba, home to Victor Ruiz, a small-town lawyer hired to coordinate the search. Nate arranges for a trip to the Pantanal region of Brazil where he thinks Rachel is probably living. Ruiz will locate guides. But besides his public task, Nate has a personal and private challenge: in Ruiz's office, he suffers his first serious bout of alcohol craving since leaving the rehabilitation center.

Nate's first try at finding Rachel occurs in a Cessna, with someone named Jevy helping him. Along with their pilot, Milton, Nate and Jevy are soon looping over *fazendas*—small farms—located on the banks of the Paraguay River. The search doesn't last long. A storm forces an emergency landing, and instead of setting the plane down safely, the pilot manages to tip it upside down in a pasture. Eventually, a military helicopter provides rescue.

Nate's next attempt occurs by boat, the *Santa Loura*. A hungover Nate boards, and the search begins. During the early stages of this try at finding Rachel, readers learn more about her past: that she is Troy Phelan's daughter by a young woman he met on a business trip to Louisiana; that she was adopted soon after birth by a family from Kalispell, Montana; that Rachel's birth mother eventually killed herself by jumping off a bridge; and that Troy met Rachel only once, right after she graduated from high school.

Meanwhile, back in Virginia, the public reading of Troy Phelan's will takes place in the courtroom. News that Phelan wrote a new will, a fact not confirmed by the portion of videotape the supposed Phelan heirs have seen, sends the family into a panic. But besides giving all of Troy Phelan's remaining money to his illegitimate daughter, the will also pays off the other Phelan heirs' debts, with one condition: if an heir contests the will, his or her debts will not be paid.

Not long after the reading of the will, Josh Stafford gets a call from Nate, who is on the Paraguay River heading toward Rachel—or at least he thinks he is. The call foreshadows problems. Sure enough, that night, a huge storm hits the *Santa Loura,* damaging it. With the boat repaired and the trip underway again, Nate takes over the helm, experiencing an epiphany. "It beat the hell out of a courtroom," he thinks. For a moment, he experiences euphoria, "shirtless, shoeless, sipping sweet coffee while leading an expedition into the heart of the world's largest swamp" (192).

When the *Santa Loura* can go no farther upriver, Nate and Jevy move to a smaller johnboat. Soon lost, they encounter a Guató tribe who tell them Rachel is living with the Ipicas, a day's ride by canoe north and west. Nate and Jevy head in that direction and eventually encounter a group of Ipica children playing in the water with their mothers. A few minutes after Nate and Jevy's arrival, the men of the Ipica tribe show up. At first, the Ipicas claim to have no knowledge of a Rachel Lane. Nate suspects otherwise, though, because one of the boys has whispered "hello" to him, evidence that Rachel may be in the area teaching English.

Tribe members eventually take Nate and Jevy to a Caucasian woman, "slender, with wide bony shoulders" (254). Guessing that she is Rachel, Nate tells her that he is there about a legal matter, that her birth father, Troy Phelan, has died. In response, she tells him that Rachel Lane ceased to exist several years ago.

So begins Nate and Rachel's friendship. During the time the two spend together, Nate begins a spiritual journey, and Rachel refuses Troy Phelan's inheritance. Before Nate heads home, Rachel pats him three times on the arm, a consecration of sorts, and asks him, "You are a good person, aren't you, Nate?" (286).

Back in Corumba, Nate is diagnosed with Dengue fever. Sometimes fatal, Dengue involves fierce headaches, hallucinations, body aches, and fevers. Nate is hospitalized and lies moaning for days, but he does recover, and upon leaving the hospital, he tries to find Rachel. Because of his delirium, he thinks he has seen her in Corumba, the image of her so strong he actually waits for her outside a small chapel.

Eventually, Nate flies back to Virginia and stays at Josh Stafford's cottage on Chesapeake Bay. There he meets Father Phil Lancaster, who enables him to continue the spiritual work he began with Rachel. After much wrangling with Troy Phelan's attorneys, Nate agrees to represent Rachel's interests during hearings about the will. To that end, he begins a letter to her. But there is a problem: where will he send the letter? He decides to mail it to World Tribes and mark it "Personal and Confidential."

Nate pays only partial attention to the legal proceedings in the Phelan matter, thinking instead about his spiritual rehabilitation. Nevertheless, he masterfully deposes Phelan family members and Phelan's servant, Malcolm Snead. Starting with Troy Phelan Jr., he exposes each person as not only profligate but also dishonest.

When Nate leaves town for a few days, Josh phones him to say he thinks that between the two of them, they can settle the Phelan estate. Josh's plan is to offer each of the heirs an amount of money—first 10 million, then 20—by way of a settlement. Eventually, Josh will offer 50 million per heir, and Nate flies to Brazil in hopes of discussing the matter with Rachel, who still hasn't been in touch. He plans to tell her that after giving out millions to Phelan's other heirs, Rachel will still have millions left to place in trust for her charitable work. For the first 10 years, only the interest on the trust will be available for distribution. After 10 years, the interest and 5 percent of the principal "could be spent at the discretion of the trustee," whoever that might be (512).

All that Nate must do is secure Rachel's signature, a task that leads to the novel's surprising conclusion.

CHARACTER DEVELOPMENT

Grisham works hard in *The Testament* to improve on characterization. Instead of the formula—young, vaguely idealistic attorney facing off against some public evil—*The Testament*'s protagonist is more interesting and more complexly depicted. Nate O'Riley is a 48-year-old has-been litigator. Once wily and tough-nosed in the courtroom, O'Riley has let years of alcohol, drug abuse, and womanizing sap his powers. When readers are introduced to him, Nate is completing another stay in a posh rehab center, wondering what life holds for him, if anything. He is, in fact, so rich a topic for exploration that Grisham devotes a key plotline to him: Can Nate stay away from alcohol? Can Nate put back together badly frayed relationships with his children? Will Nate and Rachel Lane fall in love? Can Nate define a meaningful life for himself, one that he will find satisfying? Readers of *The Testament* become as involved in finding out the answers to these questions as in learning who eventually inherits Troy Phelan's fortune.

In healing himself, Nate must overcome evil in two spheres. First, by finding Rachel, he will help undo the wrong committed by Troy Phelan.

In death, Troy has deepened the pain he has caused his family by leaving his fortune to a daughter whom he has ignored in life. But Nate himself has committed wrongs too; by choosing addiction over devotion in the past, he has brought untoward pain to his family, colleagues, and friends.

As the novel unfolds, readers can see that Nate, sadly, shares a lot in common with Troy Phelan. Both men have neglected the personal side of their lives—wives and children and home—to pursue other things. By all accounts, both have done little but work. Both are faced with angry ex-spouses. Troy's children are troubled, and Nate's will have little or nothing to do with him.

Although the two main secondary characters don't play much of a role—Troy, dead after the first few pages, and Rachel, hidden deep in the Pantanal—they are engagingly depicted. Troy's selfishness is countered somewhat and made interesting by his intelligence. Rachel's faith-based behavior remains a mystery.

Troy, in fact, resembles the despicable sitcom character Montgomery Burns on *The Simpsons*. Burns is a tycoon and careless operator of Springfield's nuclear power plant, where Homer Simpson works. Astoundingly rich, both Troy and Burns are proud of their selfishness; both are cruel to their respective toadying gofers, Smithers for Burns and Snead for Phelan. A famous Montgomery Burns quotation is "What good is money if it can't inspire terror in your fellow man?" ("Mr. Burns Quotes"). Troy Phelan rarely deigns even to speak to Snead. Early in the novel, Snead asks, "How are you, sir?" and Phelan, still narrating at this time, tells the reader, "I say nothing, because I am neither required nor expected to respond" (7).

However, other secondary characters are hopelessly flat, deserving of (and receiving) criticism. One reviewer wrote that they "have been sent over by central casting" (Pate). A second describes *The Testament*'s secondary characters as "so wooden they leak sawdust" (Bell).

In fact, Grisham tries to be comedic in his descriptions of Troy Phelan's ex-wives and six living children, creating ugly caricatures that were unnecessary. Reporting in first-person, Troy Phelan describes his eldest son, TJ, for example, as "a worthless idiot who is cursed with my name." He is "the dumbest. Though it's close" (3). A younger son, Ramble, at 14, already has "one arrest for shoplifting and one arrest for possession of marijuana" (4). From Troy's perspective, the whole lot is made up of "vultures circling with clawed feet, sharp teeth, and hungry eyes, giddy with the anticipation of unlimited cash" (4). Most reviews of the novel mention these exaggerated portraits of sloth and greed in Grisham's secondary characters. According to London's *Sunday Times*, "One does not read Grisham's works—even the best of them—for depth of characterisation and authenticity of emotion. But even by his modest standards, the portrayal of the six grasping children is careless: almost interchangeably idle and nasty, with no redeeming feelings" (Berlins).

But, as with all things Grisham, there's a mix of opinion. Deirdre Donahue thinks his treatment of the children is funny. "Grisham has a hilarious time," she writes, "detailing the messes Phelan's offspring have created by following Mammon, not God" (38). Richard Dyer, in the *Boston Globe* seconds Donahue: "Grisham lets himself have a little more fun than usual [with characterization] . . . Phelan's family is certainly grotesque" (Dyer D1).

SETTING

Although the setting of *The Testament* alternates between Brazil and the United States, much of the novel is set in the Pantanal region of the Amazon. Having visited this area in northern Brazil twice, Grisham tries hard to faithfully describe what he saw there. Through his eyes, the Amazon is both beautiful and treacherous ("With Jevy's binoculars, he [Nate] watched the shoreline for *jacarés*, snakes, and *captivaras*. And he counted tuiuius, the tall, white long-necked bird with a red head that had become a symbol of the Pantanal. There were twelve in one flock on a sandbar" [193]).

As with all things Grisham, critics disagree as to how successful his depiction of setting is. One critic wrote that "the book's best passages are those describing the jungle journey" (Berthel). Less positive appraisals include the following: "A rain forest is an ambiguous gift to a writer. Grisham's descriptions convince us that it's big, wet, green and full of anacondas and alligators but seemingly devoid of local features" (O'Brien). Richard Dyer called Grisham's depictions of the Amazon "touristy" (D1).

PLOT DEVELOPMENT

In *The Testament*, Grisham uses a carefully crafted but standard plot structure—introduction, rising action, climax or crisis, falling action, and catastrophe (Holman and Harmon 153)—to good effect. As shown in *The Street Lawyer*, Grisham's introductions are particularly strong. Still, chapters 1 and 2 of *The Testament* more than hold their own, offering enough uncertainty, blood, and surprise to keep readers' attention focused on the action. Chapter 1 introduces Troy Phelan, who complains of being "lonely and unloved, sick and hurting, and tired of living," who is in short, ready for an afterlife, if any, to come. Troy catalogs his worldwide real estate holdings and other breath-takingly huge assets. Most readers are likely jolted by Troy's list of items "owned": yachts, jets, homes, farms, islands, thoroughbreds, hockey teams—and "blondes" (2). This final word, "blondes," stated in terms of ownership, puts readers on notice. Here is a man with severe blind spots. The continuing narrative tells readers that Troy has "planned this day for a long time" (2). And when the old man dips Ritz crackers into honey and looks fondly at a can of lukewarm Fresca, which he pronounces his "final meal," questions such as "Why?" spring to mind.

Chapter 2 positions Troy (and therefore readers) on the top floor of one of Troy's office buildings, within sight of the Washington Monu-ment. Readers are told that Troy is signing the new will and that doctors and attorneys are there to bear witness to his clarity of mind and legal intentions. The will is signed, but as soon as the family, who are located literally and metaphorically "below stairs," are escorted out, Troy signs a new will. "This is my testament," the new will, Troy reading it aloud, begins, "a holographic will, every word written by me, just a few hours ago. Dated today, and now signed today . . . it revokes all former wills including the one I signed less than five minutes ago" (19). With that he "walks, almost runs" outside to a narrow terrace high above the city and then quickly flings himself over the railing. He is dead. Shocked, read-ers continue to pay attention as lawyers work to untangle the ensuing financial mess.

Most reviewers applaud this scene, considered by some "one of Grisham's all-time best openings" (Donahue). Troy Phelan's suicide is a model strategy for grabbing readers' attention and holding it well into the rest of the novel. What's odd is the narrative strategy Grisham uses to report Phelan's suicide. Phelan himself narrates the first two chapters and his jump: "Without looking below, I lunge over the railing" (20). Strange indeed—and impossible because one is dead—to both do and report.

In fact, this novel is "probably the most ambitious of the series be-cause [Grisham] has dared to vary the [plot] formula" (Dyer D1). And vary it he does, his protagonist, Nate, jaded and weary instead of eager and idealistic, only one thread of the action dealing directly with legal issues. Grisham's lawyer-hero spends most of the novel in a natural set-ting, struggling against its obstacles, instead of in courtrooms; his focus is on locating an heir, not on litigating a case. He also fights to free himself of multiple addictions. The result, according to a writer from the *Chicago Sun-Times* is that "there's a fresh energy and a new element: God." But God doesn't get in the way of a really good yarn. Grisham's "religious fervor has not dimmed [his] ability to crank out an entertaining page turner" (Donahue 38).

Several critics compare Nate O'Riley's search with that of another American popular culture icon, movie-hero Indiana Jones, but this comparison is misleading. Although Richard Dyer is correct that "a lot of *The Testament* is Indiana Jones–style action-adventure in Brazil—a form that represents new territory for Grisham" (D1), Nate O'Riley is too tired and too jaded to be much like the youthful and energetic Harrison Ford character. Indiana Jones's and Nate O'Riley's adventures may both involve physical risks, but Indiana Jones shares more in common with the young and intrepid Mitch McDeere than with the jaded Nate O'Riley.

In a manner somewhat different from earlier novels, Grisham effectively braids narrative strands across, instead of within, the chapters of *The Testament*. The story veers back and forth between Brazil and the United States, generally although not always a chapter at a time. The parts narrated in the United States deal with Josh Stafford's and others' legal efforts to settle the Phelan's estate, the parts in Brazil with events attendant to finding Rachel Lane. This continual shifting of focus propels readers forward and prevents them from tiring of Josh's legal maneuvering or Nate's physical struggle against a formidable opponent, the jungle.

Some critics have claimed that *The Testament*'s plot "creaks like a set of rusty springs" (Bell), and that "a couple of 'surprises' are dropped like anvils into the story" (O'Brien 10). Others have been charmed by what happens. Deirdre Donahue of the *Chicago Sun-Times* labeled *The Testament* "clever" (38). She and others like Grisham's premise: that a woman who stands to inherit one of the world's biggest fortunes is serving God in the Pantanal as a medical missionary; that she is difficult to find; and that, when located, she is not particularly interested in earthly wealth.

SOCIAL, HISTORICAL, AND LITERARY CONTEXTS

The Testament concerns several important social issues, not the least of which is Nate O'Riley's ability to recover from alcohol addiction. Grisham appears familiar with alcoholism and alcohol treatment—including the philosophies of Alcoholics Anonymous. His depth of knowledge shows in the discussions of Nate's background, his stay in a treatment facility, and his attempts, via Rachel Lane and, later, Father Phil Lancaster, to put his life back on track. At age 48, Nate has much to regret and repair.

Grisham also focuses on the environment in *The Testament*. He points out the ecological damage being done to the Amazon by outsiders, and he details how those seeking to profit from Brazil's natural resources are mistreating the area. Here is a typical passage, with one of Nate's guides somewhat windily speaking:

> Lots of people [want to destroy the Pantanal]. Big companies that own big farms. To the north and east of the Pantanal they are clearing large sections of land for farms. The main crop is soya, what you call soybeans. They want to export it. The more forests they clear, the more runoff collects in the Pantanal. Sediment rises each year in our rivers. Their farm soil is not good, so the companies use many sprays and fertilizers to grow crops. We get the chemicals. Many of the big farms dam up rivers to create new pastures. This upsets the flooding cycle. And mercury is killing our fish. (204)

Grisham evidently feels that U.S. citizens need to be better informed about our role in depleting the resources of the Amazon. If popular culture in the United States doesn't treat the issue very often, popular culture in the rest of the world, particularly in Brazil, does. Even films for children there have dealt with the subject (for example, *Tainá—Una Aventura na Amazonai*, released in 2001) and have a lot to say about what outsiders, particularly corporations in the United States, are doing to despoil the land.

Although Grisham doesn't single out the United States' role in depleting resources of the Amazon, he depicts Nate learning how "this ecological gem is threatened by chemical run-offs from farms, as well as plans for Hidrovia, 'a big ditch' that will link Brazil and its neighbors but will drain the Pantanal. (Trust Grisham to be timely; rain forests are old news, wetlands the new frontier)" (Pate).

Grisham also, rightly, "draw[s] attention to the plight of the Indian tribes of Brazil—a worthy objective, and an issue less commonly explored in [American] popular culture than such previous Grisham choices as child abuse, capital punishment, and the plight of the homeless" (Dyer D1). These two subplots—Nate's efforts to live a better life and Grisham's discussion of ecological and human damage being done in the Amazon—come together when Nate begins reading books about "the demise of the Brazilian Indians" (206) and begins thinking about the world around him in new, less self-absorbed ways.

But everybody can't be pleased. Some critics don't think Grisham has treated ecological issues forcefully enough. Although there may be some truth to the criticism, it is also true that focus on an issue must begin somewhere, and what better place is there than a novel that millions will already read for entertainment or when they have time to spare aboard airplanes or trains. As was noted in one review, "For such matters to emerge in entertainment fiction is a riposte of sorts to the fry 'em/nuke'em hardware catalogues offered to a vast male readership by other airport heavyweights such as Tom Clancy" (O'Brien 10).

THEMES

Although reviewers have generally rejected the idea that *The Testament* is a retelling of Joseph Conrad's modernist classic *Heart of Darkness* (Richard Dyer in the *Boston Globe* wrote that Nate's "trip to Brazil is not a voyage into the heart of darkness, exactly"), parallels are present and easy to see. Both works detail a spiritual journey made by their protagonists up rivers, into unknown territories, on continents alien to them. Protagonists in both seek someone at the behest of someone else. Both men invest a great deal of energy in finding their quarry.

Beyond those parallels, the stories are very different—even inverse, one might say. Marlow voyages up the Congo River in *Heart of Darkness*, an act that forces him to confront the "darkness" of evil in the world (colonization and the violence and theft that accompany it) and evil at the center of each human being (Kurtz and, by extension, Marlow himself). *The Testament*, by contrast, details Nate's journey up the Paraguay River into the Pantanal, a trip that leads him in more positive directions. When he reaches the heart of the Amazon, he discovers "perfect goodness" embodied in the spiritually aware and unselfish Rachel Lane. As a result of his encounters with Rachel, Nate begins healing, his life profoundly redirected.

Conrad's *Heart of Darkness* deals with the evils of colonialism. Grisham's *The Testament* only mildly treats the United States' parallel role as an economic power holding sway in the Amazon. Instead, the novel emphasizes what Grisham sees as one example of U.S. influence in Brazil: a lone medical missionary working to improve the health of indigenous people. She is much like Grisham himself, in fact, who with members of his church built houses in the area.

The titles, *Heart of Darkness* and *The Testament* highlight the books' differences. Whereas *Heart of Darkness* focuses on humankind's bleak prospects, *The Testament* sees possibility at the end of Nate's voyage. Besides being an old word for a legal will, the term "testament" also refers to the presentation of proof of the existence of something or of the truth of something. *The Testament*, then, focuses on what *is* and what *can be*, which may be why Grisham kills off the profoundly selfish Troy Phelan at the beginning of his novel and lets the recovering Nate O'Riley finish it.

Troy Phelan needs to die early in the novel if Grisham is going to deliver a positive theme. Troy is so selfish that even the gift of his fortune to his illegitimate daughter is tainted by his desire to exercise control from the grave. It is worth noting that only the daughter with whom he had virtually no contact emerges from her growing-up years with worthy morals and principles. Grisham tries to show in *The Testament* that other human beings—Rachel and, eventually, Nate—are capable of more and better than the standard set by the Troy Phelans of the world. Rachel seeks personal peace through kind acts and attention to her spiritual life. Nate, it is suggested, will follow her lead.

The Testament is, in effect, an interesting popular response to a great modernist classic. It is consolatory and hopeful, reaching a broader audience than the bleak but truthful *Heart of Darkness,* unless one counts its cinematic adaptation, *Apocalypse Now.* Casual contemporary readers who put aside *Heart of Darkness* after the first few pages of dense prose keep reading Grisham's *The Testament,* responding favorably to its optimistic message. Whether or not its assessment of the human condition is true, *The Testament* presents, as much popular fiction does, reason to look gladly toward the future and to be respectful of the human struggle to behave well.

Deirdre Donahue, writing in the *Chicago Sun-Times,* described *The Testament* as "unabashedly spiritual without being doctrinaire, a revelation that Grisham has been doing some serious searching. The major question he explores: What is needed for a man to live a good and happy life? While characters in previous thrillers have found joy in their offshore bank accounts, faith in God, not legal loopholes, is Grisham's new answer" (38). Donahue's generous reading of Grisham's *The Testament* seems right, or at least appropriately hopeful.

CRITICAL RECEPTION

Although *The Testament* was blasted by a couple of critics, its reviews were markedly more favorable than those of many Grisham works. Reviewers who like the novel appreciate Grisham's willingness to extend legal thriller boundaries. Ron Berthel for the Associated Press called *The Testament* a "pretty good tale." Despite his other complaints, the *Boston Globe* reviewer admitted, "One admires Grisham for making the effort" (Dyer D1). Bill Bell in the New York *Daily News* labeled *The Testament* a novel "that's worth staying up 'til 2 A.M. to finish."

Even those who don't care for *The Testament* have been respectful. Most of the negative reviews, for some reason, have come from Great Britain. Sean O'Brien, writing in the *Guardian*, described *The Testament* as being a "book of some humility." Still, he added, "Its presumptions are inadvertent, but none the less grating: blundering American innocence is just as unpopular as arrogant rapacity. Grisham's efforts to exceed the terms of his genre serve to expose his limitations rather starkly, and there are going to be a lot of bored and dissatisfied punters on the sun-loungers of the planet when this book gets into paperback" (10). Through the lens of hindsight, O'Brien's concerns seem not to have proven true.

5

The Brethren
(2000)

In the days preceding publication of John Grisham's eleventh novel, *The Brethren*, eager readers could access the novel's first chapter online via a free Liquid Audio player, a tool for distributing music over the Internet. They could then read the novel's second chapter and order copies, also online. When the novel's hardcover version appeared on February 1, 2000, it immediately leapt onto fiction best-seller lists. Use of Liquid Audio was Doubleday's latest technique for selling Grisham's novels. This was "the first time Doubleday . . . had released a preview using a digital download in conjunction with the print excerpt" (O'Briant).

Another event leading up to publication of *The Brethren* was the appearance in January of the first installment of Grisham's serialized novel *A Painted House*. Coming out in *The Oxford American*, a scholarly journal based in Grisham's hometown of Oxford, Mississippi, it contained a fictional account of the writer's childhood, his growing up as the son and grandson of cotton farmers in 1950s rural Arkansas. Expecting avid readers of Grisham's legal thrillers to grab up copies, the editor of *The Oxford American* increased the print run for the January issue from 50,000 to 260,000 copies (Mabe).

Grisham and the editorial staff of *The Oxford American* had reason to expect *A Painted House* would do well for the journal and for *The Brethren*.

They knew Stephen King had serially and successfully published the novel *The Green Mile* in 1996 and that Tom Wolfe had published his *The Bonfire of the Vanities* in the same way and to similar applause in 1987. About *A Painted House*, Grisham promised, "There isn't a single lawyer in the whole book," adding, "That's why I think people might enjoy it" (Mabe). Besides containing a non sequitur (people *love* Grisham's lawyers), the statement doesn't apply to the book Grisham published a month later. *The Brethren* is loaded with lawyers and judges as well as that third category of public servant, politicians.

Despite these differences, the serialized publication of *A Painted House* provided Grisham with indirect opportunities to advertise *The Brethren*. Quite simply, it ensured Grisham was part of the air being breathed at the start of the new millennium.

PLOT SUMMARY

The first of *The Brethren*'s two plot lines begins at Trumble, a minimum-security federal prison in Florida, where three former judges are incarcerated along with drug dealers, bank robbers, and embezzlers. The trio, known to their fellow inmates as the Brethren, runs numerous scams at Trumble, having put together a prisoners' court of sorts in the penitentiary library. With too much time still on their hands, the three decide to branch out beyond the prison, extorting money from married men and others who might be embarrassed for having answered personals ads in gay magazines. Posing as an attractive young gay man in a drug rehabilitation center, they begin corresponding with their victims and afterward demand money in exchange for silence. A lawyer in a nearby town helps the Brethren deposit their loot in offshore bank accounts where they plan to let it grow until their release from prison.

The second plot line concerns Aaron Lake, a widower and conservative member of Congress. Lake is a popular lawmaker and the logical choice when Central Intelligence Agency (CIA) Director, Teddy Maynard, decides to back a candidate for president, one who would work to ensure a strong military presence for the United States. Maynard feels such a presence is crucial, especially because there is considerable unrest in the former Soviet Union. With tough-minded conservative Aaron Lake in office, the CIA would have no trouble getting money and enough military power to keep Russia and other countries in line. In considering Lake as their candidate, Maynard and others at the CIA have spent considerable time looking into his background: the women he has dated since his wife's death a few years earlier and the land deal that Lake was involved in 22 years ago. Although Teddy Maynard assures Lake that his past business dealings won't be a problem, Lake is nevertheless concerned about the CIA's "sniffing through his background" (33).

And he has good reason for wanting aspects of his life kept private. Aaron is one of several men who will soon be trapped in the net strung out by the Brethren. A widower, Lake has recently begun exchanging letters with someone named Ricky, who has implicitly expressed interest in their having a sexual relationship. In fact, the letters sent to Lake are not from Ricky, but have been written at Trumble by the Brethren and have been spirited out of prison and into the mail by their attorney. If Teddy Maynard were to discover this potential for scandal, it would surely be the end of Aaron Lake's candidacy. And without Lake realizing, Maynard *is* watching him. Lake is the object of 24-hour surveillance designed to detect precisely the kinds of trouble that Lake is getting himself into.

Meanwhile, with Maynard's backing, Aaron Lake's presidential campaign is sizzling. He does well in the Arizona and Michigan primaries, but despite his successes, Lake risks trouble. One night, the Secret Service agents assigned to guard him lose sight of their man. Lake, however, only thinks he's gotten away. The Secret Service has all his doors and windows wired and transmitters in all his shoes. As they tell Teddy Maynard, "If he's not barefoot we know where he is." And that is at the post office, picking up mail from his private mailbox. Surveillance tightens as Teddy Maynard directs his men to find out why Aaron Lake sends and receives mail in such a suspicious way.

"Ricky," the young man writing to Aaron Lake, is, of course, a figment of the Brethren's imaginations. Presumably a patient at Aladdin North, a Florida drug rehabilitation center, he tells Aaron that he works out daily and spends hours improving his tan. His letters to Aaron, who uses the pseudonym Al Konyers, express loneliness and yearning. Teddy Maynard's government spies intercept one such letter from Ricky to Al. Within hours, Teddy Maynard and his CIA operatives know that "Ricky" is former judge Hatlee Beech and that money is motivating the imprisoned judges.

By this point in the campaign, Teddy Maynard would find it too difficult to stop the successful presidential campaign he has set in motion. Aaron Lake is almost sure to win his party's nomination. The best Maynard can do is head off Aaron's potential problem with Ricky. To find out where Lake hides his private mail, he directs his staff to have Ricky send Al Konyers an audio tape with a small transmitter in its casing. Once Al puts this tape with his other correspondence from Ricky, Maynard's men will be able to get at and destroy any potentially damaging mail in Aaron Lake's possession. But this particular effort on Maynard's part is unnecessary. The agents find the tape in the garbage, which is where Aaron Lake evidently files all of his mail from Ricky. News of Aaron's careful behavior is a relief for Teddy Maynard. Aaron, meanwhile, realizes the political stakes are now too high to risk getting caught in a scandal. He decides to end his correspondence with Ricky.

Before he can do so, however, potential disaster strikes. On a flight from Pittsburgh to Wichita, the plane Aaron Lake is on catches fire. He is asleep when the trouble begins, having written several thank you notes and the letter ending his relationship with Ricky in the minutes before drifting off. When he awakes to smoke, fumes, and darkness, Aaron stuffs all the letters he has been writing into his briefcase. Fortunately, the pilots manage to vent the cabin and land the plane safely in St. Louis.

At first, Aaron's near tragedy appears not to have had repercussions—that is, until the Brethren receive a thank you note for being a campaign volunteer. This is their tip-off that they have a bigger fish on their hook than they realized. The note is signed by Aaron Lake, whose handwriting is identical to that of Ricky's friend Al. The Brethren smell riches greater than they've previously imagined.

Aaron Lake, meanwhile, is making great strides in his campaign for the presidency. After the Pennsylvania primary on April 25, he nearly has a lock on a nomination. Realizing that his secret mailbox may cause him embarrassment, he instructs a campaign volunteer to close it and leave no forwarding address. At Trumble, a new prisoner, Wilson Argrow (real name, Kenny Sands, a member of the CIA), checks in. His job is to keep track of the Brethren and to find out how much they know about Aaron Lake.

Before Aaron Lake gets his Mailbox America box closed, a letter, intercepted by a surveillance team, arrives from Trumble. This letter does not mince words. It is from former justice Joe Roy Spicer and demands money and release from prison in exchange for silence about Lake's sexual interest in young men. Before the situation achieves resolution, adventures occur, and people die. Readers follow along as Teddy Maynard pits his intelligence against the minds of the Brethren. Will Aaron Lake become the next president of the United States, or will the Brethren manage to ruin him? What will happen to the Brethren once the resources of the CIA are arrayed against them? Because no one's morals are above reproach and no right cause is being protected, one wonders how Grisham could possibly lead his characters to a satisfactory conclusion.

CHARACTER DEVELOPMENT

According to most discussions of storytelling, characterization and plot are linked. "The actions (including verbal discourse as well as physical actions) are performed by particular characters in a work, and are the means by which they exhibit their moral and dispositional qualities. Plot and character are therefore interdependent critical concepts—as Henry James has said, 'What is character but the determination of incident? What is incident but the illustration of character?'" (Abrams 159).

Grisham, however, puts this definition to the test. Events in *The Brethren* are compellingly plotted, but characterization is sparse. Although, as has already been established, Grisham's fame has never been based on his ability to create round (that is, thoroughly depicted and believable) characters, this novel, perhaps more than any of his others, offers virtually nothing in the way of compelling characterization. As one reviewer phrased it, Grisham's major characters are little more than "a series of verbal identikits" (Taylor). Although Grisham provides readers with quirky details about his main characters—Hatlee Beech suffers from hemorrhoids (11), Finn Yarber's wife "had a gray butch cut and hair under her arms" (97), short and fat Joe Roy Spicer runs the scams, Aaron Lake's cholesterol hovers at 160, and Teddy Maynard speaks seven languages (22)—the details never lead to a full picture of, or a modicum of sympathy for, any of them. Things happen to characters, and characters do things, but that's where it all ends. One reviewer asked, "Who can get excited by characters this shallowly drawn and this transparently wicked? They don't even seem to have fun being bad" (Dyer).

There is certainly not a sympathetic protagonist in *The Brethren*, even though Aaron Lake at first seems to be a typical John Grisham hero. He is, after all, male, professionally competent, young to middle-aged, and white, like Grisham himself. Although readers sense he has a spiritual life, he, like most of Grisham's protagonists, is not actively religious. For 14 years, Lake has served as a congressional representative from Arizona. He is a widower "with a quaint little townhouse in Georgetown that he was very fond of" (20). He only occasionally takes part in the D.C. social scene. Beyond these demographics, readers learn that he likes to drive himself to work, listen to classical guitar music while stuck in traffic, be alone, and receive preferential parking. What readers aren't privy to are his feelings. Grisham resolutely keeps these to himself.

There is little to cause readers to be interested in or care about the Brethren either. Joe Roy Spicer, a former justice of the peace in Mississippi, is in prison for skimming profits off bingo at a Shriners club. Finn Yarber, former chief justice of the California Supreme Court, received five years for tax evasion. Hatlee Beech, a federal judge from east Texas with a drinking problem, "ran over two hikers in Yellowstone," both of whom died (12). None of the three appears to regret his misbehavior or is reflective about his life in any other way.

The Brethren's victims in their sexual scam are as opaque and only slightly more engaging. Grisham devotes parts of chapters to their stories. All of them are older men who have secretly answered ads from the same "Ricky," whose ad Aaron also responds to. There is a jewelry store owner named Curtis (real name Vann Gates); an Iowa banker called Quince; someone named Coleman Lee who runs a Gary, Indiana, taco stand; and a man named Brant from Upper Darby, Pennsylvania. And then there is Al Konyers, better known as Aaron Lake. As soon as the fictitious Ricky establishes a firm connection with each man—detailing his many problems and sounding eager to meet—a message quite different from previous ones gets sent, this one with extortion as its goal. "Ricky" demands money in exchange for not telling the families of his victims what their family member has been up to. As with the Brethren and Aaron Lake himself, readers never learn enough about any of these characters to care what happens to them. The only way readers might become engrossed in their stories is via catharsis, Aristotle's term for the way in which "many tragic representations of suffering and defeat leave an audience feeling not depressed, but relieved or even exalted" (Abrams 331). The stories of Curtis, Quince, Coleman, Brant, and Al serve as a reminder that the path of secrecy and dishonesty is slippery and downward. It is difficult to reverse a direction once one has embarked on it. Witnessing the development of this theme in *The Brethren* lets readers experience increasing tension, fear, and then resolution, followed by relief if not exaltation.

PLOT DEVELOPMENT

What is interesting about *The Brethren* is that, despite its weak characterization, the power and intricacy of Grisham's plot seem to compensate. Although *The Brethren* may not contain Grisham's most compelling plotline, what *is* there ensures that most readers will finish the book, some enthusiastically. This time, Grisham develops two separate plot threads, gradually draws them together, and then braids them. Chapter 1 introduces the Brethren: who they are, how they came to reside at Trumble penitentiary in northern Florida, what they do to pass their days. Chapter 2 presents Aaron Lake and Teddy Maynard, both of whom live in Washington, D.C., and sets the stage for Lake's presidential run. Chapter 3 returns to Trumble, outlining the Brethren's most recent moneymaking scam.

In chapters 4 and 5, however, Grisham gradually begins pulling these threads together. He details Teddy Maynard's surveillance of Aaron Lake. Then, in a separate section of the chapter, he introduces readers to the Brethren's lawyer. Trevor Carson visits the Brethren at Trumble, and readers can see how money and correspondence related to the scam come into and out of prison. In chapter 5, Aaron Lake announces his candidacy for president, and readers learn more about one of the Brethren, Hatlee Beech. By juxtaposing these two plot lines without letting them touch, Grisham raises questions and, in the reader, tension. How and when will the stories merge?

Although readers might be expecting that blending to occur in chapter 6, Grisham subverts their expectations. He introduces a new character, Quince Garbe, whom the Brethren are blackmailing. Married and wealthy, Garbe has a lot to lose if someone can show he has a sexual interest in a male pen pal. This segment of chapter 6 sits beside one that discusses Aaron's presidential campaign.

For the next six chapters, Grisham continues with this plotting strategy: cutting from Aaron Lake's campaign to the Brethren's antics at Trumble and from Teddy Maynard's behind-the-scenes manipulations of Aaron Lake's campaign to trips made by the Brethren's attorney to the Bahamas to deposit the Brethren's blackmail money in a safe offshore account. Meanwhile, Grisham keeps readers' attention by showing the heinous lengths—including murder—Teddy Maynard is willing to go to get his candidate elected. To refocus readers' attention on the Brethren's scam, Grisham periodically introduces a new victim.

Not until chapter 13, nearly halfway through the novel, when Aaron Lake escapes from his house to gather mail from a secret mailbox, do the separate plots begin to twine. The letter Lake picks up is one the Brethren have written; the trio from Trumble has unwittingly snagged a whale. Grisham, of course, has hooked his readers at this point. Those still with him will most certainly read to the end.

THEMATIC ISSUES

One theme of *The Brethren* concerns the politics of democracy, which Grisham surely regards as dangerously corrupt. Nothing about Aaron Lake's campaign is above board. The Director of the CIA is managing it— and people's opinions—in order to accomplish his own goals: maintaining the United States' military supremacy and seeing to it that weapons do not get into the wrong hands. Although such goals may seem understandable, Maynard's methods of achieving them are not. Rigging an election is bad enough, but Maynard does worse things. He forces a candidate, Dan Britt, out of the election by threatening blackmail, the same method used by the Brethren to extort money from their victims. In Britt's case, Maynard tells Britt that he knows that Britt has an illegitimate child in Bangkok. Maynard also knows how Britt financed trips (through taxpayers' money) to Thailand to visit the child's mother. As Grisham says,

> Teddy had dirt files on hundreds of politicians, past and present. As a group they were an easy bunch to trap. Place a beautiful young woman in their path, and you generally gathered something for the file. If women didn't work, money always did. Watch them travel, watch them crawl in bed with lobbyists, watch them pander to any foreign government smart enough to send lots of cash to Washington, watch them set up their campaigns and committees to raise funds. Just watch them, and the files always grow thicker. He wished the Russians were so easy. (75)

Grisham shows how one person with an endless supply of money and connections can shape the future of the United States and, for that matter, the world.

A second theme of *The Brethren* is that privacy in America is a myth. Anyone can find out anything about anybody and use it for his or her own gain. Americans have been folded, spindled, and mutilated for decades, but we have continued to assume—in the face of substantial evidence to the contrary and the ubiquity of computers—that our individuality, our privacy, on some level is safe. Grisham disabuses readers of that myth, demonstrating that no one—not the candidate for president of the United States, not any person on the street—can keep private information that anyone else wants to know.

A third theme of *The Brethren* concerns American homophobia. Grisham wrongly leaves readers to assume, as one critic puts it, "that the [gay] victims of extortion are getting what's coming to them, if only because they're closeted" (Dyer). Grisham portrays gays and gay relationships as pathetic. Besides, it is hard to imagine that a wealthy bank president and the Brethren's other marks would risk everything to receive innocuous little notes from someone like Ricky. The letters exchanged are superficial; the only feeling mentioned is loneliness. The sexual innuendo is banal. "I'm much leaner now, and tanned. They let us tan for up to two hours a day here, weather permitting. It's Florida but some days are too cool. I'll send you another photo, maybe one from the chest up. I'm lifting weights like crazy" (140).

LITERARY AND PHILOSOPHICAL CONTEXTS

Far more than any of Grisham's earlier novels, *The Brethren* assumes an existential worldview. Like much so-called serious modern literature, several of John Grisham's novels—especially *A Time to Kill, The Firm, The Rainmaker,* and now *The Brethren*—lend themselves to existentialist readings. That is, Grisham focuses in those works on a modern world that is chaotic and meaningless and, in all but one, on heroes who struggle to make sense of a world out of which no sense can be made. Although existentialist thinking is a key component of modernism, Grisham depicts in *The Brethren* a simpler, darker, more contemporary version of that philosophy.

Beginning in the mid- to late nineteenth century, existentialist philosophers wrote that humans drift alone through a senseless world. Compounding their isolation, these hapless drifters make life decisions despite there being no reliable set of rules or objective codes of behavior enabling them to choose wisely. And choose they must, for the only thing worse than choosing what might be called a "wrong" course of action is choosing no action at all. Existentialist philosophers agree that, even though there is no such thing as "truth" (or "right" or "wrong"), we get closest to truth—and our lives come closest to being fulfilled—when we act enthusiastically despite the hazardous consequences of such action. Those who are dominated by—or, worse, become paralyzed by—indecision have lost the battle before the war begins. In the existentialist's world, life is all about choice: choosing and living with the choices we have made, being responsible for them. In a chaotic world, people acting responsibly represent the only possible order there is.

In employing existentialist themes, Grisham links his novels to great works of modernism. Fyodor Dostoyevsky's *Notes from the Underground* and Franz Kafka's *The Trial* and *The Castle* are early examples. Among French writers, Albert Camus, Andre Malraux, and Jean Paul Sartre wrote notable existentialist texts. In Great Britain, the novels of James Joyce, Virginia Woolf, D. H. Lawrence, and Evelyn Waugh, among many others, showed the influences of existentialism, and in America, much of the traditional canon of the twentieth century proceeds from an existentialist base. Of Americans, Ernest Hemingway is perhaps the most frequently cited example of a writer presenting existentialist themes. In his novels—ranging from *The Sun Also Rises* to *The Old Man and the Sea*—one can trace an evolving code of conduct for existential heroes: act despite uncertainty; face the world bravely if alone.

Like most popular fiction in the legal thriller genre, John Grisham's novels reflect this existentialist thinking. In *A Time to Kill* (1989), the chaotic world is embodied by bigotry against African Americans. When two white men rape an African American female child, Tonya Hailey, the rapists receive a sentence of life plus 20 years, but are scheduled for parole after just 13 years. By contrast, when the rape victim's incensed father, Carl Lee Hailey Jr., guns down the two, the father appears headed to the gas chamber.

Jake Brigance, an existential hero who represents the rape victim's father in court, chooses to withstand the prejudices of his community in order to defend Carl Lee Hailey. Although he is successful, the townspeople burn his house and do their best to destroy him professionally. Jake stays the course, eventually securing justice for Carl Lee.

In *The Firm* (1991), young lawyer Mitchell McDeere combats evil within a wicked microcosm: the law firm he has recently joined. Bendini, Lambert & Locke offers McDeere a high salary, a BMW, and a beautiful home in exchange for his work. He accepts until he discovers the company earned its wealth through illegal activities, money laundering among them. Although they risk dying to do so, McDeere, his wife, and a friend collect evidence against the firm and thereby topple at least one modernist temple of evil.

By the time Grisham published *The Rainmaker* (1995), he seemed less assured that a single hero could put a dent in the world's wickedness or bring down evil institutions. Rudy Baylor, Grisham's young lawyer hero, combats wrongdoing, this time in the form of an insurance company that unfairly refuses to pay for a lifesaving treatment for one of its insured. Although Rudy establishes in court that his client, Donny Ray Black, deserves a bone marrow transplant to treat leukemia, Black is dead—beyond help—and the company successfully argues it cannot afford to pay the fines leveled against it. At novel's end, Baylor has left the law, no longer believing it can be a force of good in a corrupt society.

In *The Brethren*, Grisham's dark portrait is of an existential world lacking heroism in any form. There is in *The Brethren* no Jake Brigance, no Mitchell McDeere, no Rudy Baylor, to combat disorder. Chaos runs rampant. In the view Grisham presents in *The Brethren*, the world of presidential politics contains as much evil as does a prison. There is no single evil empire against which a hero can struggle: Teddy Maynard, the director of the CIA, is willing to commit dishonest acts to establish himself and the United States in powerful positions, just as the Brethren are willing to trick the world's weak and vulnerable for the same reason. Aaron Lake, who in an earlier Grisham novel might have stood up to Teddy Maynard and resisted Maynard's efforts to buy him the election, not only allows the purchase to take place, but also is one of the weak and lonely men being blackmailed by the Brethren.

It is unsurprising that reviewers of *The Brethren* wondered upon the book's publication what had happened to the gritty moralism of John Grisham and complained about the novel's lack of heroes. A postmodern world—one lacking a Jake Brigance, a Mitch McDeere, or a Rudy Baylor—is light-years darker than the existentialist stance of modernism. Instead of a heroically existentialist piece, Grisham has written a typological narrative in which characters, "like figures in an allegory, do not change or develop but reveal themselves in response to the demands of a situation" (Tompkins 92)—and reveal themselves darkly in this case. The situation is existential darkness, but with Lake letting it happen.

CRITICAL RECEPTION

Although reviews of *The Brethren* were mixed, several were no-holds-barred positive. The London's *Independent* labeled the novel "all absolutely brilliant," adding that "from the most unpromising material Grisham spins out a compelling, in places beautifully written, thriller" (Thorne). The *Daily News* of New York judged the novel "light-hearted yet suspenseful, quite entertaining throughout" (Connelly), and the *St. Louis Post-Dispatch* said it "finds . . . [Grisham] in top form . . . [doing] what he has shown he can do best: put desperate people into desperate situations, then let them find ingenious ways to do unto others before the others do unto them" (Singer). Even the *New York Times* was unequivocally positive, the reviewer referring to the novel's "steady action" and "clever surprises" (Goodman). The *Times-Picayune* also praised *The Brethren*: it is "fast-paced and action-packed—and cannily timed" (Larson). This reference to timing is important. *The Brethren*, published on February 1, 2000, focuses on a fictionalized U.S. presidential campaign, walking readers through the primaries, the national conventions, and the election. Early readers of Grisham's novel thus got to experience two campaigns simultaneously: the imaginary one between Aaron Lake and his opponent, Governor Tarry; and the real 2000 campaign between Al Gore and George W. Bush.

Most reviews of the novel, however, contained both praise and criticism. Cleveland's *Plain Dealer* noted Grisham's "admirable skill in juggling his many characters, their many motives and the multitude of actions inspiring the reactions that keep the story moving" (Sandstrom). But today's readers expect more; they want "humor. Maybe a hero. Maybe even a pretense of depth"—all of which this reviewer found lacking (Sandstrom). The *San Francisco Chronicle* reviewer offered grudging accolades. The novel "doesn't stink." It is even "occasionally diverting" (Kipen). However, its biggest problem, according to the reviewer, is its "utter lack of a hero, or an anti-hero, or even a lovable loser. Great works of fiction can get by without a single redeemable character, and often do. Great works of popular fiction, with very few exceptions, can't" (Kipen). The *Toronto Star* also equivocated. Grisham exhibits his "natural authority" in the writing, an authority that convinces readers "that, yes, this is the way things are done at high levels of government. Yes, this is what it's like in such a prison. Yes, some people will pour their souls out in compromising letters to men they've only met in the pages of a singles 'zine," but this novel's "gaping flaw" is that it lacks a hero of any sort (Heller).

A second review in the *Independent* lauded Grisham's handling of "factual details," saying they are presented with "crisp efficiency," but it objected to the novel's weak characterization. "The plot makes the Pink Panther seem a miracle of realism and the prose clatters over repetitions and cliches like a train over a set of points" (Taylor). The *Los Angeles Times* reviewer commented that *The Brethren* is "one of Grisham's leanest" works, but found the world of this novel dark to the point of being "wearisome." "A novelist has to love the world," the reviewer added—"although he may hate many of its features—and has to like his characters enough to make them interesting. When faced with such flat and universal contempt, even fans as devoted as Grisham's may start to wonder whether this contempt extends to them too" (Harris).

A few reviews were undiluted by any praise. *USA Today* commented that *The Brethren* is "utterly devoid of . . . page-turning pep. Sad to report, reading *The Brethren* is like trudging through wet cement in a stiff, cold breeze" (Donahue). A reviewer for the *Buffalo News* couldn't get beyond an implausible element of plot: "Like it or not, many novel writers rely on the one-in-a-million coincidence to goose along their plots. But get this: The fateful envelope [a letter from the Brethren to their mark] passes through the staked-out, much-burgled post office box without the CIA opening it. These top-notch operatives were even steaming open the Publishers Clearing House packets, by Grisham's description, and the one piece of mail they couldn't afford to miss gets by them. Darn" (Galarneau). The *Boston Globe* objected on ethical grounds: "The [book's] moral lines are crazed, and there's not even an elementary sense of rough justice in play. The book isn't exactly homophobic, but it makes it seem that the victims of the extortion scheme are getting what's coming to them, if only because they're closeted" (Dyer).

6

A Painted House
(2000)

Readers of *A Painted House*, John Grisham's semiautobiographical coming-of-age novel set in Arkansas in the 1950s, probably won't learn many new details about people in the author's early life. As Grisham coyly admits, "One or two of these characters may have actually lived and breathed on this Earth, though I know them only through family lore, which in my family is a most unreliable source." Grisham is equally evasive about events in the novel. "One or two . . . may indeed have taken place, though I've heard so many different versions of them that I believe none of them myself" (Dyer). In short, it is dangerous to assign *too* much autobiographical significance to Grisham's tale of a boy's life.

In fact, the decision by Grisham's publishers to print 2.8 million copies for *A Painted House*'s first run must have been difficult, falling as the book does between so many cracks. "Consider the faces of the elite Doubleday staff as Grisham, their prize cash cow, ambled into the office with a coming-of-age manuscript; imagine their frenzied meetings, afterward, as they racked their brains as to how to market and sell the book" (Crosbie). In fact, Doubleday's confidence in this particular crossover experiment is downright astounding. The company printed as many copies of *A Painted House* as it had of each of Grisham's five previous thrillers (Kinsella 178).

Publicizing the novel involved a two-step strategy. First, Doubleday did something it hadn't done before with a Grisham work: it printed galleys as "advance reading copies" (Kinsella). Along with the galleys came a letter from Grisham, acknowledging "this is not a legal thriller" and offering the tantalizing possibility the novel *might* be autobiographical (Kinsella).

Second, Grisham arranged to have *A Painted House* published serially in *The Oxford American,* a well-respected literary journal and winner of the Utne Reader's Alternative Press Award for General Excellence in 1999. There were also early reports that the book would be made into a movie, rumor enough to entice many on-the-fence readers into buying or borrowing it. A well-worded statement from Grisham's publicist fueled the flames of possibility, along with a cautionary, yet tantalizing disclaimer that "the deal is not done yet. We should be making a statement shortly" (Kinsella). Although a Hollywood blockbuster never materialized, a modest made-for-television version appeared in 2003, scripted by Patrick Sheane Duncan. The movie received an award for sound mixing, and its young star, Logan Lerman, earned a nomination for a Young Artist Award.

Although Grisham claims he made no effort to market *A Painted House* differently from his previous novels, Doubleday's publicity staff admit to some shifts in sales strategy. Grisham made a "rare public appearance" at the New York Public Library. He also went on the *Today Show.* An article in the Life section of *USA Today,* a segment on NPR's *All Things Considered,* and an interview with Larry King suggest that Grisham might have been more invested emotionally in this book than in earlier novels. There were also online promotions on Doubleclick, Epinions, and Salon (Kinsella).

THE PLOT

A Painted House is set in the Arkansas Delta during September and October 1952. An unidentified narrator gradually reveals himself by referring to "my father" and "Pappy," the grandfather. By the third page, readers know that seven-year-old Luke Chandler is telling the story.

As the novel begins, Luke and his grandfather, Eli Chandler, are driving into nearby Black Oak to find Mexican laborers willing to help them harvest their cotton. Luke's family members are not wealthy landowners. They rent their land and live barely better than the people they hire at harvest time, working alongside them in the field. The Mexican harvesters have traveled, uncomfortably, across the country via open trailer as part of the annual harvest migration. As soon as they take the job, they set up housekeeping in the Chandlers' barn. Luke's grandfather also hires a family of so-called hill people to work the harvest. The Spruills—scraggly folks from the Ozarks—agree to the job, moving tents and crates onto the Chandlers' front lawn. Among the Spruill children is a brutal adult son named Hank, a disabled boy named Trot, and a daughter, Tally, whom Luke is especially taken with. She is 10 years older than Luke and pretty.

The harvest gets underway. Up before dawn, Luke and his family eat ham, biscuits, and sorghum. Then they pile onto a tractor-pulled wagon with the Spruills and the Mexicans for a hard day's work. At night, the family gathers around the radio to hear Harry Caray call Cardinal baseball from St. Louis. One of the Chandlers is not at home for the cotton harvest. Luke thinks often of his uncle, a young man named Ricky, who is away fighting in Korea. Like the rest of his family, Luke worries about whether Ricky is safe.

On Saturdays the family picks cotton only half the day. They spend the rest of the day in town, visiting friends from other farms and going to the movies at the Dixie Theater. One Saturday, a fight breaks out behind the Co-op, the local grocery and gathering spot. Fighting occurs there regularly, and although Luke is forbidden to go near the area, he sneaks there anyway and witnesses Jerry Sisco, one of a family of "dirt-poor sharecroppers," facing off against a hill person by the name of Doyle (56). When Doyle appears to be getting the worst of the deal, Hank Spruill, the oldest son of the family camped in the Chandler front yard, steps in and whacks Jerry hard. Even though Jerry's two brothers try to defend him, they are no match for Hank, who throws them to the ground. The next day at church, Luke learns that Jerry has died, probably from blows received in the fight.

On Sunday, the town deputy, a heavy-set man called Stick, arrives at the Chandlers' to question Hank. The Chandlers, the Spruills, and Stick meet under a pin oak on the front lawn. Stick interviews Hank, who admits only to having broken up an unfair fight. When Stick asks whether there's a corroborating witness, Hank tells him Luke saw what happened. Cast suddenly into the spotlight, Luke corroborates Hank's lie that the murder weapon was first picked up by the victim himself. Having been taught that "lying would send you straight to hell" (76), Luke promises himself he will confess his sin to God "as soon as I could" (77).

An opportunity for confession doesn't come that afternoon. Instead, the Chandlers carry food to some poor neighbors, the Latchers, who are rumored to have an unwed pregnant daughter. Townspeople want confirmation of the pregnancy and, if possible, the name of the father. The Latchers, however, keep the errant daughter hidden away, and the Chandlers leave without completing their mission.

The next week, Luke and his mother take baskets of vegetables to the Latchers. Luke's mother hopes to reach the Latcher place early enough to catch the rest of the family in the fields and the pregnant Libby at home, confirming the town's suspicions about a baby. But Mrs. Latcher greets Luke and his mother and immediately presses the latter into service. Libby is in labor; there is no way to keep her pregnancy a secret any longer. When Luke's mother urges Mrs. Latcher to get the doctor, Mrs. Latcher says no. Calling the doctor would only advertise the family's shame. In a compromise, Luke and his mother race to get Luke's grandmother, who is a midwife. Luke's parents and grandmother hustle back to the Latchers to help poor Libby.

The Latcher secret, for the time being, belongs only to the Chandlers—and to Tally Spruill, who convinces Luke to spill what he knows when Luke first returns from the Latchers' house. Tally then talks Luke into sneaking with her into the Latcher yard to witness the birth. Tally is mesmerized by what they can see from their hiding place; Luke is more concerned about being discovered and spanked for his disobedience. The baby takes a long time to arrive. Luke falls asleep and then awakens to hear Libby Latcher's final yells and the emerging infant's first squalls. Luke and Tally hustle home, barely ahead of Luke's family. Luke manages to curl up on a bedroom floor, apparently asleep, before his parents step wearily into the house.

At supper the next day, the Chandlers entertain a surprise guest, Percy Latcher, one of Libby's brothers. He has disturbing news: the Latchers believe Luke's Uncle Ricky is the father of the new baby. The Chandler men move off to the porch. The women feed Percy, who is red-eyed and half starved. They all guess Percy could be right. Another visit to the Latcher household occurs, this time with Pappy in attendance. They realize that in delivering a poor sharecropper child, Gran may have delivered her own grandchild.

One subplot of *A Painted House* crosses several chapters and begins when Luke and his mother discover someone is painting a small strip on the east side of their farmhouse. Whoever is doing the job apparently wants to remain anonymous. At first, no one tries to figure out what is going on, and the painted portion of the house gradually expands. Eventually, the Chandlers realize that little Trot Spruill is the painter. Proof comes one day at the hardware store, where Luke's mother learns that a crippled boy and a girl from the hills have bought paint with the girl's picking money.

In October comes news that Grady Sisco, the brother of Jerry Sisco, has escaped from prison. Having been jailed for murder, he is thought to be hiding at home and planning to avenge his brother's death. Stick comes out to the Chandler place to warn everyone, especially Hank, that Grady poses a threat. But Grady doesn't get there fast enough. One evening, Luke's father, realizing that the Spruills are as sick of Hank's bad behavior as he is, tells Mr. Spruill that Stick plans to arrest Hank. Before long, Luke is awakened by the sounds of angry voices out on the lawn. Creeping outside and into a field across the road, Luke witnesses Hank arguing with his parents, who tell him to leave. Listing for them all the people he despises in Black Oak, including members of his own family, Hank stuffs a duffle bag and heads on foot up the road. Before Hank can get farther than a nearby bridge, however, Luke sees one of the Mexicans, a man nicknamed Cowboy, whom Hank has also mistreated, attack him. The fight doesn't last long. Hank throws a jar of something at the Mexican, and a knife flashes. Hank receives a stab wound first in the stomach and then another and another. When the fight is over, Cowboy pushes Hank's body off the bridge into the water below.

Luke tries to sneak back to his house without being seen, but before he reaches the yard, Cowboy jumps him, still wielding the knife. He warns Luke that if he tells anyone what he has seen, he will kill Luke's mother. When Luke's parents awake in the morning, they find their son scratched, bleeding, and terrified under their bed.

But the river is rising, and it eventually floods the unharvested crops. Tally, the object of Luke's affection, runs away with Cowboy and dispirited, the Spruills decide to go home. Luke's mother and grandmother pack food for the Spruills' trip back north, and Trot Spruill turns over his paintbrush and paint to Luke. Soon, Luke has picked up where Trot left off, doing a job no Chandler has done before him. Watching the paint coat the house's unprotected siding feels good to Luke, who realizes he would prefer a life of painting to one picking cotton.

CHARACTER DEVELOPMENT

Grisham proves in *A Painted House* that he is capable of creating more fully developed characters than he has in any of his legal thrillers to date. The Chandlers are engaging and convincingly described. As the first-person narrator, Luke Chandler is especially well developed, although Luke's mother, grandparents, and other secondary characters are effectively portrayed too.

Luke Chandler

Grisham does a good job of depicting events from the perspective of seven-year-old Luke Chandler. He also believably captures a child's feelings about the larger, looming world. Doing so must have been an intriguing exercise for a writer who has generally stayed outside the heads of his thriller protagonists.

Luke is a delightful character who learns from his parents and grandparents that hard work is honorable and that home and family are strong buffers against indifferent nature and the world's occasionally damaged inhabitants. He has also internalized his family's example that kindness to others is key to living well. As even Luke's father and crotchety grandfather know, humans are at their best in a community, and happiness is dependent on the well-being of others.

Grisham shows Luke enjoying what typical seven-year-old boys of his time and geography would. He gobbles up St. Louis Cardinals baseball games on the radio, is excited by the prospect of watching television, is mesmerized by the chance to peek at naked Tally Spruill, and looks forward to the summer carnival and other activities in Black Oak.

And Luke is tested. During the six weeks covered in the novel, he is tempted to keep secrets from his parents and to lie, both acts considered sinful by the Baptist church, which he and his family attend. He also experiences more than nearly any seven-year-old would in so short a time. He witnesses sexual intercourse, the birth of a baby, and not one, but two, murders.

Grisham seems less concerned about *how much* happens to Luke and more concerned about Luke's overall believability as a narrator. As he says in an interview, "The biggest challenge was to keep [Luke] as a seven-year-old. I think at times the kid's a lot smarter than any seven-year-old would be. I kept stretching it, I kept asking myself how much would a kid know and remember and see" (Kinsella).

Reviewers who see flaws in the novel's character development have usually pointed to this problem: Luke, they say, seems too wise for his age. One reviewer observed that Luke narrates as if he has "read *Tobacco Road, The Grapes of Wrath,* and *To Kill a Mockingbird,*" adding that the child ("one tough little kid") seems to have survived "a major attack of literary symbolism" (Dyer). Another reviewer cautioned more mildly,

"We should probably forgive the author for making him a tad too precocious" (Slater).

A reviewer who complained about Luke's style of speech was probably on target. According to him, "Luke has a stiff, off-kilter prose style, and an ear not precisely attuned to the rhythms of common speech" (Dyer). As an example, he cites the following passage: "The Sears, Roebuck & Company catalog came in a brown wrapper, all the way from Chicago, and was required by Gran to be kept at the end of the kitchen table, next to the radio and the family Bible. The women studied the clothes and home furnishings. The men scrutinized the tools and auto supplies. But I dwelt on the important sections—toys and sporting goods" (Dyer).

Other characters in the story treat Luke as if he were older than he is. At the store, the proprietor asks Luke whether his parents are planning to move north. What follows is a monologue an adult is unlikely to have directed at a child, even a special one: "I hear," says the proprietor, "some of the boys are already makin' calls, tryin' to get on at the Buick plant. They say the jobs are tight this year, can't take as many as they used to, so folks are already scramblin' to get on. Cotton's shot to hell again. Another good rain and the river's over the banks. Most farmers'll be lucky to make half a crop. Kind of silly, ain't it? Farm like crazy for six months, lose everything, then run up North to work and bring back enough cash to pay off debts. Then plant another crop" (245).

Although a case can be made that Luke is an autobiographical version of his creator, Grisham both discourages and encourages such comparisons. For example, he makes Luke seven in 1952, three years before he himself was born in 1955. On the other hand, Grisham admits to picking a lot of cotton as his characters do, and "the setting is very accurate. That house and that farm and that town are very similar to my grandparents' house and farm and the town of Black Oak, where I spent the first seven years of my life" (Kinsella). Besides, Luke narrates like a budding writer would. Confessing to his mother that he spied on Libby Latcher having her baby, he tells readers, "I embellished here and there, to help move the story and build tension, but for the most part I stuck to the facts. She was hooked" (269).

Luke's Family

Grisham creates a realistic, hardworking, and warm family for Luke. His mother "is loving and understanding, and quietly strong." His grandfather "is stubborn and proud, a bit of a male chauvinist who fears no man but is afraid of his feelings" (Berthel). The relationship between Luke's grandparents feels right, with the grandmother, gritty, standing up to her husband when she deems it necessary. The gentle class struggle between Luke's mother, who was raised in a "painted house," and his father, who was not, is also convincingly portrayed.

The Spruills and the Mexicans

Grisham is also writing at his best when he creates the dirt-poor Appalachian Spruill family. They have a gently comic quality about them that is reminiscent of the down-and-out Bundrens in William Faulkner's *As I Lay Dying*. Hank Spruill is mostly villainous, in contrast with Trot's damaged virtue.

Except for Grisham's more complicated portrait of Cowboy, who eventually murders Hank Spruill, the Mexican farmworkers are depicted as ennobled, if "all small and skinny and dirt poor." Although the Spruills sprawl with their junk in the yard, the Mexicans neatly occupy the barn. Although the Spruills snip at each other, the Mexicans get along. Luke's mother gives them the best vegetables from her garden, a sure sign they are among the elect. Unlike the Spruills, they get into comparatively little trouble. Only Cowboy misbehaves, and Tally—a Spruill who flirts with him—may be partly responsible for his poor judgment.

Not everyone thinks Grisham's portrayal of Mexican farmworkers is positive. One reviewer mentioned Grisham's "liberal tone (Luke's mother is concerned at the treatment of migrant workers)," but says Grisham goes on "to be unspeakably offensive at the same time: The Mexicans spill through the book smelling badly (they have 'a particular odour'), cooking tortillas and laughing like imbeciles" (Crosbie).

PLOT DEVELOPMENT

A Painted House covers six difficult weeks in the Chandlers' lives, and Grisham's careful plotting enables readers to experience several moral and ethical quandaries faced by Luke. One reviewer described *A Painted House* as "a beguiling and gracefully constructed novel" (Dugdale).

If there is a complaint to be made about plot, it may be that too much happens in too short a time One critic described the narrative as "snaking" (Crosbie). In the course of 294 pages, "Luke has watched an assignation, learned of an elopement, peered through the window during a childbirth, and witnessed two murders, not to mention surviving a series of natural disasters that include a flood and a tornado" (Dyer). So much action strains the reader's obligation to achieve "a willing suspension of disbelief," that is, their ability to let go and accept the story as really true.

That said, Grisham does a laudable job of weaving together at least four plotlines. The first concerns the farm and whether the Chandlers will be able to harvest their cotton and continue the work the family has done for generations. A second plotline involves strangers—the Mexicans and the Spruills—who come to town and whether they will adjust well to their new surroundings and get along. A third concerns class issues and the Latchers' new baby. Here the struggle is between the Latchers, who are among Black Oaks' profoundly poor, and the Chandlers, who have a foothold, however tentative, into middle-class life. Finally, Luke himself and his moral and spiritual growth make up the fourth, and most important, plotline. Readers want to know whether Luke will develop into a good and kind adult, especially in light of recent events, all of which might harden him. Too bright to accept benignly his lot in life as the son of a poor Arkansas cotton farmer, "Luke chafes against the drudgery of the fields, all the while experiencing emotions that form his character: love and hatred" (Nebenzahl).

It is interesting that the climax of the novel involves flooding, an event of biblical proportions and significance. In the Chandlers' case, the family's farming future is cast into doubt when the rains come and the creek on their property rises. The flood that washes away their cotton crop is, in many ways, the final blow, causing the next generation of Chandlers, Luke's parents, to plan to leave the farm for a job in the industrial North.

SETTING

Grisham is particularly good at depicting setting in *A Painted House*. Of course, he is working with material he remembers well: the environs of Black Oak, Arkansas, where he spent his early years. Even so, one can only praise him for his sensual depictions of place and for eliciting, in readers old enough, memories of a time gone by. As one reviewer noted, "The sights, sounds, smells and tastes of the time and place ring with an authenticity Grisham doesn't even strive for in his other books; they convince here because he doesn't have to strive for them—they are part of the warp and woof, the texture, of memory" (Dyer). Grisham does especially well with food, for example, when he reports on a sumptuous picnic of fried chicken, heaping bowls of fresh vegetables, corn bread, potato salad, and peanut butter ice cream made by an elderly lady from town.

SOCIAL AND CULTURAL CONTEXTS

Nostalgia

Like Harper Lee's *To Kill a Mockingbird* and Rick Bragg's *All Over But the Shouting,* among others, John Grisham's *A Painted House* provides a nostalgic look backward at the American South. Although each book focuses on a different decade (*To Kill a Mockingbird,* the 1930s; *A Painted House,* the 1950s; and *All Over But the Shouting,* the 1970s), all three time periods are depicted in similar ways and viewed through a child's eyes. Whatever the hardships people faced, there were powerful compensatory moments. In *A Painted House,* those moments often involved baseball and the radio. As Luke fondly and frequently recalls, "After supper, we took our places on the porch as Pappy fiddled with the radio. The Cardinals were at Philadelphia, playing under the lights. Musial came to bat in the top of the second, and I began to dream" (61).

Poverty

A Painted House looks at levels of poverty. Nearly everyone in the novel is poor, but some people are poorer than others. First are the Mexicans, forced to migrate across the United States to harvest crops in an effort just to survive. Second are the Spruills who haven't driven as far as the Mexicans, but whose poverty is nearly as deep. With all their belongings stuffed onto their truck, they are prepared to stop anywhere someone offers to put them to work. Then there are the Latchers, neighbors of the Chandlers. Dysfunctional and defeated, they are so poor they have lost the ability to even try to better their lives.

From the perspectives of the Mexicans, the Spruills, and the Latchers, the Chandlers look wealthy, but readers know otherwise. The Chandlers' future depends on the success of their cotton crop. They owe money at the local cotton gin, at the John Deere dealership for tractor parts, and to other businesses for fuel and seed and supplies. The novel's title, *A Painted House,* speaks powerfully about the tightened belts of Black Oak, Arkansas. Although a painted house would be nice, there is no money for brushes or color. The Chandler farmhouse exterior, therefore, remains bare, with weathered boards, and a painted house remains a dream. The difference between the Latchers and the Chandlers is that the Chandlers haven't quit trying. Luke's relatives still believe in the American dream: that hard work will eventually result in a measure of material success.

To create tension around the issue of poverty, Grisham depicts Luke's mother, Katherine, as coming from comparative wealth. That is, she has lived in a painted house, and she resents conditions at her in-laws' home. As Luke says, "My mother vowed to herself that she would not raise her children on a farm. She would one day have a house in town or in a city, a house with indoor plumbing and shrubs around the porch, and with paint on the boards, maybe even bricks" (50).

Class

Class struggles occur in *A Painted House*, even though Grisham doesn't identify them as such. The citizens of Black Oak tolerate both murders in the novel because outsiders of lower station die, not people like themselves. In the fight behind the Co-op, Hank Spruill kills Jerry Sisco, in part "because nothing electrified Black Oak like a good fight" (56). Jerry Sisco's death is local entertainment, blood sport the religious townsfolk can later shake their heads over and deny any involvement in. To them, Hank's and Jerry's lives appear to matter less than those of local God-fearing Baptists and Methodists. Hank Spruill is an Appalachian "hillbilly" who owns no land and has few prospects. Jerry Sisco is one of a family of "dirt-poor sharecroppers who lived less than a mile from town" (56). His family has already gained a reputation for class-related violence. Last year, Luke hears, "Billy Sisco had almost killed a Mexican in a fight behind the gin" (57).

Like Billy Sisco, Hank Spruill has also been in trouble with the Mexicans. He throws dirt clods against the barn to bother them, and when one man, Luis, opens the barn door to see what's going on, a clod hits and hurts him. Hank also strikes another of the Mexicans, Cowboy, with a baseball. Cowboy's lacerations are not only physical but also emotional. Aware that in any class hierarchy, Mexicans have even less power than the local poor or Appalachians, Cowboy doesn't seek immediate revenge. He gets it later, when he murders Hank and pitches his body off a bridge on the Chandlers' property.

The Chandlers are also embroiled in a class struggle—with the Latchers—and Grisham gives the families sound-alike names to underscore the precarious similarity of their stations in life. Luke is very clear that plenty of distance separates his family from its poorer neighbors. That Luke's Uncle Ricky, away at war in Korea, may have impregnated Libby Latcher before leaving belies that claim. Luke is not a party (and, therefore, neither are readers) to discussions that surely went on in the Chandler home about Ricky's unwise and, given class differences, shameful behavior.

It is interesting that no black people appear in Grisham's novel of an American South in the 1950s. For whatever reason, poor whites and Mexicans seem to have done the menial farmwork in this part of Arkansas and participated in the class-inspired power struggles that are an integral part of most heterogeneous small-towns.

Although he is only seven, Luke is aware of class issues, without being able to articulate exactly what "class" means. According to the Chandlers' unstated hierarchy, they are at the top, followed by the Spruills, who are poor out-of-towners, and then the Mexicans, who are poor and foreign. When, the year before, Luke got sick after eating the Mexicans' tortillas and salsa, Luke's grandmother blamed his illness on the Mexicans' lack of hygiene.

Not everyone accepts the Chandlers' implied class hierarchy. Hank Spruill ignores the low status ascribed to him. He gives Luke orders— once to bring him ice water from the kitchen—and although Luke knows that Hank's doing so violates some unspoken rule, he does what Hank says. Even when Hank taunts Luke—accusing the child of being uppity, mocking the Chandlers for living in an unpainted house—Luke doesn't tell his parents. Luke's silence makes sense. If he tells on Hank, his grandfather will pick a fight with the Spruills, his father will back up the old man, and the Spruills will leave. If that happens, Luke will have to harvest more cotton to make up the loss. Better to keep silent, he reasons, and he does.

THEMES

Coming of Age

A Painted House is a coming-of-age tale, or bildungsroman. Even though the novel covers a short span of time, six weeks, it deals with seven-year-old Luke's intellectual, moral, spiritual, social, and psychological development. Always a sensitive child, Luke learns a great deal from events that occur during the cotton harvest of 1952. In telling Luke's story, *A Painted House* sits beside well-known classics of the genre: *A Portrait of the Artist as a Young Man* (James Joyce), *Huckleberry Finn* (Mark Twain), *Great Expectations* and *David Copperfield* (Charles Dickens), and *Siddartha* and *Steppenwolf* (Herman Hesse), as well as popular, more contemporary bildungsromane: the Harry Potter series (J. K. Rowling), *To Kill a Mockingbird* (Harper Lee), *Anywhere But Here* (Mona Simpson), and *All the Pretty Horses* and *The Crossing* (Cormac McCarthy).

As happens in such novels, certain lessons are reinforced while others are learned for the first time. Luke is reminded, for example, that his parents' and grandparents' values are solid ones: their faith in the goodness of all people, their sense of responsibility that requires they take care of their neighbors, and their commitment to hard work and individual responsibility. Luke learns, however, that no matter how good he and his family are, the world—both human-created and natural—will determine the extent of their success. He will be pummeled by the children of the neighbors whom his family is trying to help (the Latchers); people will try to kill each other, often successfully (Hank, the Siscos, and Cowboy); and the floods will come. Further, he learns that staying and struggling may not be the best course of action. Grisham seems to suggest that it is wise for Luke's parents to flee the South, trading in the unpredictability of farming for jobs up north.

As often happens in bildungsromane in general, especially southern ones, Luke's education begins with his seeing things he isn't supposed to see. "The child who witnesses disturbing events is a time-honoured motif in Southern fiction, and Luke's forebears stretch back to Tom Sawyer and Huck Finn, who see Injun Joe commiting [sic] murder" (Dugdale). Nevertheless, in the tradition of the bildungsroman, Luke isn't permanently damaged by the view. To the contrary, he grows wiser to the indifferent ways of the world. He also learns that good and evil as well as other tidy dichotomies are not as neat as they may have appeared. The killer isn't wholly evil nor the victim totally good.

The Example of Trot Spruill

An intriguing subplot in *A Painted House* concerns the not-just-right Trot Spruill. Whether he is mentally disabled or physically crippled or both, Grisham doesn't say. Still, it is Trot who, after managing to be excused from picking cotton, starts putting the first coat of paint on the Chandler farmhouse. Grisham never explains why Trot chooses this form of self-expression. Is he an artist metaphorically crippled by a world in which he is condemned to hard manual labor? Or is he a retarded child just looking for something to do?

Trot brings to mind one of Southern literature's most famous characters, Benjy Compson in William Faulkner's *The Sound and the Fury*. Described by Faulkner as an "idiot," Benjy nevertheless narrates the first section of Faulkner's famous novel and shows himself capable of extraordinary sensitivity. Despite his mental problems, Benjy proves to be the strongest and kindest of the Compson children, surviving in a world that leads his brilliant older brother Quentin to suicide and his beloved sister Caddy to moral ruin.

On a smaller scale, Trot Spruill might teach parallel lessons. By getting out of farmwork and by beginning to paint the Chandler house, Trot shows Luke the value of beauty, of persistence, of wily wisdom.

What Is the Good Life?

Grisham wisely does not answer this question, leaving readers to puzzle it out based on their own readings of *A Painted House*. On the one hand, the Chandlers embody the good life for their time and circumstance. They eke out a living without compromising family values. In the process, they delight in the pleasures (church services, baseball, carnivals, ice cream, and television) afforded them by Black Oak's intimate small-town life. Grisham questions, though, whether such pleasures are enough, considering how hard the Chandlers must work to earn them and in light of the precariousness of farming. They are without a safety net and always just one flood or one drought away from disaster.

Ultimately, the good life that Luke recalls may be possible only in memory, which may be why Grisham found this novel so important to write. Memory allowed him to rejoice in the positive and to recontextualize the negative through art.

In breaking his chain of 11 legal thrillers, Grisham joins other popular writers who have temporarily shifted genres or subjects for reasons of nostalgia. Tony Hillerman, for example, "interrupted his Navajo mysteries to write *Finding Moon* [set in the Philippines], and David Baldacci . . . took a break from thrillers . . . with the publication of *Wish You Well* . . . which, as a period novel set in the rural south, carries parallels to *A Painted House*" (Kinsella).

Still, some reviewers don't appreciate Grisham's nostalgic but "very momentary departure from the legal books" (Kinsella). As one sniffed, "Like an unfilled, restless multi-millionaire on a Picasso buying spree, Grisham is turning to art for consolation and the kind of prestige generally denied an heir to a trashy novel fortune" (Crosbie). Another observes that *A Painted House* proves Grisham is like other "fabulously rich people these days." Instead of haughtily ignoring the rest of us, they seem to "worry about being misunderstood. Making huge sums of money isn't enough any more. What the really rich really want is to be well thought of" (Yanofsky).

CRITICAL REACTIONS

A Painted House earned more good than bad reviews. Those who like the novel have said it is pleasurable reading. They tend to see *A Painted House* as "evocative" (Nebenzahl), "gentle," and, in a good sense of the word, "sentimental" (Berthel). Others have applauded the book for its "sincerity" and its "likable" qualities (Dyer). One reviewer wrote, "There is much to recommend this . . . thoughtful novel . . . There is an attention to detail here—from the descriptions of the arduous task of picking cotton to an affectionate recollection of the simple joy of listening to a baseball game on the radio—that is absent from the going-through-the-motions plot of *The Brethren*" (Yanofsky). "It could be his most thrilling [novel] yet," claimed a reviewer who has not always had positive things to say about Grisham's legal novels (Millar). Another wrote that it is a "good yarn whose pages are turned with ease" (Bolt).

Those who don't care for *A Painted House* have criticized what others have praised. One reviewer claimed that the good parts are too deeply buried beneath a "sleepy, meandering collection of rural stereotypes," adding, "the author seems intent on delivering an upright and safely predictable past in which [Grisham's] readers can take comfort" (Maslin). Others wrote their reviewers with a foul edge, one observing that the story "is told with all the nuance and liveliness of an animatronic Mark Twain, with a malfunctioning robotic mouth" (Crosbie). This reviewer questioned, unfairly it seems, why "the novelist chose to humiliate his own past this way, that his publisher allowed its modest emperor to appear before us, unclothed" (Crosbie).

7

Skipping Christmas
(2001)

Skipping Christmas arrived in bookstores around Thanksgiving of 2001, an early and, for many, a surprise entry into the holiday book market. In writing a Christmas-themed story—one with absolutely no thriller components—Grisham joined other celebrities ringing in (or cashing in on) the holidays. The most critical of Grisham reviewers, Lynn Crosbie of the *Toronto Star*, wrote, "Grisham's novel plays a significant part in the pre-Christmas menace at large. Its timely, snow-dappled cover, I'm sure is screaming out to thousands of stress-racked, inspiration-starved shoppers, who need only to make the leap from 'Hey, Dad liked that *Pelican Brief*' to 'What a perfect gift idea.'"

Regardless of the public's reasons for buying *Skipping Christmas*, buy it they did. Appearing a mere month before the end of the year, Grisham's Christmas fable—or short (at 177 pages) holiday narrative that makes a moral point—was a best-selling work of fiction for 2001 *and* for 2002, selling well over a million copies each year. Grisham's publisher even went so far as to predict *Skipping Christmas* would become "a modern Christmas classic."

It is easy to see why reviewers and others regarded Grisham's move into the Christmas market with a jaundiced eye, one person commenting, "Christmas books are gifts that keep on giving—to writers" (Fretts). The typical best seller has a year's shelf life before being put on backlists or taken out of print. "But a shrewdly written and marketed Christmas trifle can sell year after year and support its author all through old age, long after writer's block has stopped the creative arteries" (Kisor).

PLOT SUMMARY

Skipping Christmas concerns a middle-aged couple, Luther and Nora Krank, and, indirectly, their daughter Blair. When Blair joins the Peace Corps and is assigned to Peru, the elder Kranks realize they will be alone for Christmas for the first time in many years. Something of a curmudgeon, Luther doesn't care for Christmas anyway. When his wife says Christmas won't be the same without Blair, Luther agrees.

And, indeed, it appears it won't be. Luther, a tax accountant who keeps close track of things financial, obsesses about the $6100 that he, Nora, and Blair spent on Christmas the year before. Suddenly, Luther has an idea. If he and Nora were to skip Christmas, they could take a 10-day cruise in the Caribbean and still come out ahead. Within a day or two, Luther stops at a travel agency, coming away with brochures and pamphlets about a ship called the *Island Princess* and a cruise that would take the pair to the Bahamas, Jamaica, and Grand Cayman. Although Nora resists his plan to cancel Christmas completely, saying that at least they mustn't forgo their charitable giving, Luther persuades her a cruise is better than Christmas alone without Blair. He also convinces her they can't skip Christmas only halfway. They must go all the way.

In the days that follow, Luther doesn't make any preparations at all for the holidays. At work he announces via letter that he and Nora will not be exchanging presents with anyone. When Boy Scouts come to the door selling Christmas trees, Luther refuses to buy one.

For the first time in memory, the Kranks are not a part of the neighborhood team hoisting a decorative Frosty the Snowman onto their rooftops. For years, Hemlock Street, where the Kranks live, has scored high in the annual citywide holiday decorating contest, even being rated best decorated and best lit. Without the Kranks' participation though, Hemlock finishes sixth. A photograph of the Kranks' unlit house appears in the paper next to an article about Luther and Nora's decision to skip Christmas. In the article, an unidentified neighbor accuses the two of "a rotten display of selfishness" (91).

Everything changes on Christmas Eve, however, when they receive a call from Blair. Although they've assumed their daughter is patiently ministering to the indigenous people of Peru, she is in Miami, she says, and is flying home. She is in love, she tells her parents, and will arrive shortly with her fiancé, a Peruvian physician named Enrique. Blair tells her parents she wants Enrique to see a typical American Christmas, just like the ones she experienced every year growing up.

Luther and Nora have only a moment to stare at each other, no time for accusations or recriminations. From this point on, Nora sets the rules. Of first importance, Blair is never to know about the cruise they must cancel. This key rule established, Luther's job is to find a tree. With all the tree stores nearly depleted, Luther hands over $75 to the Boy Scouts in a Kroger parking lot. The tree he gets for his money has scarcely a needle left on it.

Nora is off on her own round of errands. She leaves behind a guest list for the party they are suddenly having, on it names of old friends who will accept a simple apology and come to a celebration. Inviting friends to the party gives Luther another idea, this one for the Christmas tree. The Trogdons across the street are leaving for a ski trip on Christmas Eve. Luther appeals to Wes Trogdon to borrow their tree while they are gone.

While Nora is at the grocery, Luther slips on a patch of ice on the roof in his rush to get Frosty into position. Luther and Frosty careen toward the eaves and concrete below, and Luther hears Frosty hit the ground. But electrical cords twine around Luther's feet, and after he rolls off the roof, he finds himself dangling upside down off the side of his house. While one neighbor calls 911, others crowd beneath Luther in case they must break his fall. Nora arrives just as an ambulance screeches onto Hemlock.

After an airborne Luther is freed, the Kranks confess their predicament. Good friends that the neighbors are, they are soon involved in arrangements for Blair's party. When Blair and Enrique arrive at the airport, the police give them a stylish escort to the Krank home. And Enrique's welcome into the Krank family goes off without a further hitch.

CHARACTER DEVELOPMENT

"More of a fable than a work of fiction" is how one reviewer described *Skipping Christmas* (Roberts). That one sentence says plenty about characterization in Grisham's Christmas tale. Fables, by definition, focus on lessons to be learned, not on people, and that is precisely what *Skipping Christmas* does. Only Luther Krank emerges as a real human being; Nora and the neighbors play slight supporting roles.

Luther Krank

The novel's protagonist is an anal tax accountant—a tautology some would say—who knows to the dollar how much he and his family spent on Christmas the previous year—$6100, or, as he puts it, "nine percent of my adjusted gross!" (14). Krank whines incessantly about money:

> $6100—$6100 on decorations, lights, flowers, a new Frosty, and a Canadian spruce; $6100 on ham, turkeys, pecans, cheese balls, and cookies no one ate; $6100 on fruitcakes from the fireman and the rescue squad, and calendars from the police association; $6100 on Luther for a cashmere sweater he secretly loathed and a sports jacket he'd worn twice and an ostrich skin wallet that was quite expensive and quite ugly and frankly he didn't like the feel of. On Nora for a dress she wore to the company's Christmas dinner and her own cashmere sweater, which had not been seen since she unwrapped it, and a designer scarf she loved, $6100. On Blair $6100 for an overcoat, gloves and boots, and a Walkman for her jogging, and, of course, the latest, slimmest cell phone on the market. (13–14)

The litany continues for more than a page. Luther Krank's name says it all. It suggests he has the sternness and sense of purpose of a Protestant reformer and a "cranky" disposition to boot.

It is easy—even, tempting—to conflate Luther Krank and Ebenezer Scrooge, especially considering that Doubleday's press release for the book promises Skipping Christmas is "certain to become as timeless and beloved a classic as A Christmas Carol and The Grinch" (Fretts). Here is Ebenezer reassigned to the twenty-first century in the body of a bean counter named Krank. One critic even calls Krank the "professional and literary descendant of [the] countinghouse squire . . . but without Scrooge's entire disdain for Christmas and all the good things it means" (Guinn). The words that follow "but" are the important ones. Luther Krank is by no means Ebenezer Scrooge. He is somewhat genial, if a little crabby. He is not as selfish as Ebenezer, but he is cynical and snippy—maybe a bit like Grisham himself.

It is equally easy to see Luther Krank as Dr. Seuss's Grinch. Witness Grisham's singsong Seuss-like catalogs ("no clutter and wrappings, no traffic and crowds"). Unsettled by his daughter's departure for Peru, Luther Krank determines to steal other people's holiday. Nora is emblematic of the Whos, the dear little people who live at the bottom of the Grinch's mountain, who return every act of malice with kindness.

On the other hand, some readers think Krank comes off as a sympathetic character, especially when "he has to hide in his basement to escape his seemingly fascist neighbors" (Pate). He may also seem sympathetic when he eats crow with those same neighbors so that they'll help him create a last-minute holiday celebration for Blair. In short, readers working overtime to empathize see him as "just an ordinary guy who has stepped in one too many slushy puddles and opened too many meaningless gifts" (Pate).

Still, Luther Krank is an engaging character for a fable: "a well-drawn mess of ill temper and petty crabbiness" (Nguyen et al.). He embodies a lesson for others whether or not he masters the lesson himself.

Nora Krank

Many female readers may see themselves in Luther's wife, Nora. She is an agreeable woman who struggles to support her husband's whims where skipping Christmas is concerned. Nora herself would *never* ignore the holidays, but she is willing to accommodate her husband's desires, if for no other reason than that she has done so repeatedly in other matters for at least 20 years.

Although Nora is an essentially flat character, a *type* as opposed to a fully realized human being, her role as accessory to Luther's "crime" of ignoring the holidays is important to the novel. Nora is already in the midst of Christmas preparations—she is at the grocery buying chocolate for baking—when the scheme occurs to Luther: "how nice it would be to avoid Christmas . . . A snap of the fingers and it's January 2. No tree, no shopping, no meaningless gifts, no tipping . . . no fruitcakes, no liquor and hams that no one needed, no 'Rudolph' and 'Frosty,' no office party, no wasted money" (10).

To Nora's credit, she resists Luther's efforts to ignore Christmas completely, saying that at least they mustn't forgo their charitable giving. Beyond that, she is the dutiful wife, doing as her husband directs her. When someone calls to see if she is ready to place her usual order for Christmas cards, her response is unequivocal: she and Luther will not be sending out cards this year. She also goes on a diet with Luther and accompanies him to a tanning salon so that they will have a good base coat of fake tan before the cruise.

Nevertheless, she periodically wavers in her commitment, for example, when Luther won't let her answer the door to carolers. In silent protest,

Nora heads to the shower as the singing starts outside their door, the only way she can stand to ignore the voices echoing faintly from her front porch. Friends target Nora more than Luther with their silent criticism. After a tanning session at the mall, Nora runs into the family's minister, who mentions having heard that she and her husband are about to go on a cruise. There is no stated criticism, but the message is clear. Her conscience is also pricked when she learns one of their neighbors has cancer and may be celebrating her last holiday. That fact and the crank Christmas cards featuring Frosty arriving daily from around the country—Luther guesses the cards are a joke being played on them by a neighbor—also give Nora pause.

Once Blair announces she and Enrique are on their way home, Nora experiences a change of heart. She becomes more assertive, and Luther acquiesces. Having laid down certain rules, Nora modestly decorates the inside of the house and heads out to gather supplies for the last-minute party she and Luther will host in Blair and Enrique's honor. Of course, there is the small matter of guests. Who will still come to a Christmas Eve event at the Kranks, especially when they've so thoroughly alienated all their friends and neighbors? In the peanut butter aisle at the grocery, Nora desperately invites to the celebration an acquaintance whose name she can't even think of.

Although there is no direct parallel with Nora in Dickens's *A Christmas Carol*, Luther's wife comes closest to resembling the amiable Bob Cratchit. Like Ebenezer Scrooge's loyal employee, Nora does her best to make others happy.

PLOT DEVELOPMENT

Grisham narrates *Skipping Christmas* from a limited third-person point of view: Luther Krank's. The novel is well plotted in that the story is engaging, "elements of plot fit together nicely," and "characters pass through . . . obligatory stages of conflict" (Roberts). Certainly, Grisham brings some well-honed storytelling skills to his little Christmas tale, marshaling his talents as a writer of legal thrillers to increase tension and packing the story with entertaining tidbits. As well, there is "pathos" and "gentle satire" (Minzesheimer). Thanks to these elements, readers aren't likely to put down the novel before finishing it.

But there are parts of the plot that seem conventional, forced, even banal. The reviewer who said the plot is "entirely predictable" is probably right (Crosbie). For example, it doesn't take a professional literary critic to foresee that Blair will be coming home for the holidays. Another critic, Charles Spencer for the London *Sunday Telegraph,* complained that the Kranks' efforts to reschedule Christmas after having canceled it are a "cop out." Spencer wanted Krank to remain heroically "Scrooge-like," an act that seems counterproductive to Grisham's goal of writing a warm, and profitable, "Christmas classic." Still, the behavior of the Kranks' Hemlock Street neighbors when Luther and his wife reveal they won't be hoisting Frosty onto their roof for the holidays is implausible. No decorating contest could possibly explain the neighbors' fury when the Kranks announce their change of plans. The hate mail, the newspaper criticism, and the icy glares simply don't have a realistic feel, even for those living in the smuggest and most closed of American suburbs.

SOCIAL AND CULTURAL CONTEXTS

Skipping Christmas presents Grisham's own satirical glimpse of suburbia in the United States: look-alike neighborhoods dominated by "grim conformity and complacency" (Spencer). Although there may be some truth to Grisham's portrayal, it seems somehow dated, as even the hinterlands and midsections of the country have grown more diverse, if, in some cases, grudgingly. Neighborhoods such as the Kranks' may still be out there—free of Jews, Buddhists, Hindus, or Muslims; free of blacks and Asians and Hispanics whose differing religious or cultural practices need accommodation or, better, celebration—but they are increasingly rare. Simultaneously waning is the expectation that whatever one family in a neighborhood does must be imitated lockstep by everyone else, causing Luther's "act of defiance with huge consequences" to seem petty, silly, and more 1950s than twenty-first-century America (Roberts).

Besides, for all its criticism of suburbia, the novel tends to uphold white, middle-class prejudices rather than subverting them. One reason Enrique is welcomed into the Krank family with such affection may have to do with his skin color and economics. Blair has told her parents that Enrique is handsome, but Luther is especially relieved to find his daughter's fiancé is "two shades lighter than . . . himself!" (167). Enrique also speaks perfect English, having been "educated in London" (168). In short, "except for references to a black Santa at the airport and a Pakistani family who moved away, the Kranks' world is as white as the snows of yesteryear" (Pate).

THEMES

The Importance of Christmas

In an effort to avoid giving *Skipping Christmas*'s saccharine ending away, reviewers barely mention the novel's main theme: that the rituals of Christmas play more significant roles than we realize. Luther Krank appears to master this lesson after stridently resisting it, learning Christmas's importance when he must quickly muster a celebration for his daughter Blair and her new fiancé. He also sees love's power over him in the person of that daughter. He spends not a minute weighing options when he learns Blair wants a special holiday at home.

Mindless Materialism

That "mindless materialism" surrounds Christmas is a truism some Americans annually ignore. In *Skipping Christmas,* Luther is obviously within his right to regret spending so much money during the holidays, but he is wrong to try to cancel his family's celebration. He is also wrong to stand in judgment of his neighbors' careless spending that is very similar to what his own, until very recently, has been. Certainly, the neighbors' glum reaction when they hear the Kranks are going on a holiday cruise suggests they might be jealous or angry, or they might feel they themselves are being judged. They might even be questioning the Kranks' decision to spend the money they've saved by canceling Christmas on a fancy trip to the Caribbean. Certainly, there is enough malice in their behavior to suggest they have nearly lost sight of the goal of the holiday: the expression of love, acceptance, and generosity, which in the end they nevertheless manage to offer up to the Kranks.

And what more can be said about "mindless materialism" that hasn't already been said, and said well, in countless other works of fiction? America's seemingly insatiable desire to own more and better "is such a familiar target that one could knock it down with a snowball. Instead, Grisham calls in smart bombs and bunker busters. Such a misanthrope is Krank that even Ebenezer Scrooge would mutter 'Lighten up, man!'" (Kisor).

Whether Luther really learns his lesson after Blair's telephone call is unclear. True, he seems to realize his neighbors are kind and will help him in a pinch. Nevertheless, at the end of the novel, he seems not to have grown spiritually, emotionally, or ethically as a result of events that have occurred. Standing outside in the cold night air, he reflects on having nearly died in the fall from his roof and on his friends and neighbors who canceled their Christmas Eve plans to help Nora and him out. Suddenly Luther is "starving, as usual" and then lusting after smoked trout. "'I'll eat a fruitcake too,' he vowed to himself. Skipping Christmas. What a ridiculous idea. *Maybe next year* [italics mine]" (177).

MOVIE VERSION

Like nearly all of Grisham's books, *Skipping Christmas* seems to have been ready-made for adaptation to the screen. Although many expected it to become a made-for-television movie like *A Painted House,* a feature-length film renamed *Christmas with the Kranks* was released on November 24, 2004, by Sony Pictures Entertainment. One critic mentioned Arnold Schwarzenegger for the role of Luther Krank "bungling the decorations and falling hilariously off the roof," but Tim Allen got the part, with Jamie Lee Curtis playing Nora, and Dan Akroyd as a neighbor.

All in all, the movie adheres to Grisham's plot rather closely, although the screenplay, by Christopher Columbus, shows Jamie Lee Curtis unclothed (described by reviewer Snyder as "the Worst Nude Scene of 2004"), a moment not detailed in the book. The movie also exaggerates the "Tong War [that] unfolds against [the Kranks] whose only crime is not getting in the holiday spirit." As one reviewer wrote, "From that point on, I could not buy all the fuss. Do people act this way? Anywhere on planet Earth?" (Snyder).

Christmas with the Kranks did not do well with reviewers, receiving a mere five fresh to 119 rotten reviews, as of February 2007, on the Rotten Tomatoes Web site (www.rottentomatoes.com/m/christmas_with_the_ kranks/). Film reviews on the site accused the movie of being "flat-footed" (*Orlando Sentinel*), "humbug" (*Arkansas Democrat Gazette*), "meretricious claptrap" (*Movie Mom at Yahoo! Movies*), and even "evil" (*Greenwich Village Gazette*), this latter interesting criticism, perhaps, carrying over to the novel. The world that both movie and novel depict is smugly closed. Little wonder critics have used the term "fascist" to describe it.

CRITICAL RESPONSES

Positive reviews of *Skipping Christmas* were only *mildly* positive, as if reviewers concluded, "Well, it *is* the Christmas season." Those liking the book described it as "readable and amusing" (Kiser), "relatively pleasant" (Ogle), "entertaining" (Pate), "pleasant, if packaged" (Minzesheimer), and "amusing if predictable" (Pate). The plethora of "pleasants" and "ifs" set the tone.

Negative reviews mention *Skipping Christmas*'s heavy-handedness (Kisor) and excess fat (Fretts). A common complaint is that the story is trite, "an odd mixture of tension, suburban comedy and schmaltz" (Mazmanian). As one writer concluded, "Grisham's prose is so labored, his satire so clunkingly superficial and obvious, that you would hardly wish it as a present on your worst enemy" (Lively).

It is fitting that the imagery used to criticize the novel often involves fruitcakes, especially given that the novel "appropriates the bizzaro world mood of an existential nightmare," in which people behave strangely against a backdrop of meaninglessness (Mazmanian). "Nutty as a fruitcake," we say. Thus, when critics pick up on the image—"Grisham mostly trades in stale fruitcake jokes and sub–*Christmas Vacation* slapstick" (Fretts) and "the story is meant to nurture the soul but, like the fruitcakes so dreaded by the Kranks, it is artificially sweet and full of pits" (Roberts)—well, it's caveat emptor, or, in this case, let the *reader* beware.

Those in the book industry behind Grisham's decision to publish a Christmas classic seemed to hope *Skipping Christmas* would become a ritual read on a par with *A Christmas Carol*. Although Grisham's *A Christmas Carol*–esque theme seems pleasant and comforting, the book is too obvious and bland to invite yearly rereading. Still, even though one critic warned, "Don't look for *Skipping Christmas* from Christmas 2002 onward," there it was at Borders and Books a Million in 2005, its bright blue covers crying out for purchase (Kisor).

8

The Summons
(2002)

After two years of sojourning in the land of literary fiction, John Grisham returned in 2001 to the legal thriller genre that made him famous. On February 2, 2002, Grisham published *The Summons,* a novel renewing loyal readers' acquaintance with tightly plotted fictions about lawyers—some upright, some sleazy, some only slightly oddball. As with Grisham's previous few books, Doubleday released a printing of 2.8 million copies of *The Summons,* which sprang quickly onto best-seller lists and entered *USA Today's* weekly Top 150 Best-Selling Books list a mere two weeks after its arrival at bookstores. It remained on the list a total of 53 weeks, even briefly hitting the number 1 spot, as all but four of Grisham's novels have. By March 31, 2004, it had also become one of *USA Today's* top 100 best-selling books, attaining a rating of 33, ahead of *The Runaway Jury* (40), *The Chamber* (45), *The Partner* (52), *The Street Lawyer* (53), *Skipping Christmas* (60), *The King of Torts* (80), and *The Client* (90) and behind *The Testament* (24), *The Brethren* (27), *A Painted House* (31), and *The Rainmaker* (32).

THE PLOT

Professor N. Ray Atlee is a solitary man, a 43-year-old professor at the University of Virginia School of Law in Charlottesville, Virginia.

Divorced, childless, and his mother dead, Ray is not particularly close to his eccentric father, who lives on the old family estate in Clanton, Mississippi. He doesn't get along with his younger brother, Forrest, a drug addict and all-around ne'er-do-well either. Ray seems happiest when he is either jogging, which he does regularly, or flying a small Cessna airplane he rents at an airport north of town. His dream is to "lease a Bonanza and disappear into the skies" (16).

A letter from Ray's elderly father gets the novel underway. The father, a retired judge, sends both his sons a formal summons—thus the novel's title—requiring them to be present in his office on Sunday, May 7, at 5:00 P.M. Judge Atlee indicates he wants to "discuss the administration of my estate" (4). Ray finds the letter puzzling because his father, as far as he knows, has no money to leave to either of his sons. His salary as a judge in Mississippi has not been particularly large, and whatever money he has accumulated, he has given away or used to pay for Forrest's unsuccessful drug rehabilitations.

To keep the appointment with his father, Ray drives 15 hours westward in his new Audi TT roadster. Arriving in Clanton, Ray discovers the old man dead on the sofa in his study. Because he doesn't want to notify the authorities of the father's death until Forrest gets there and because he doesn't know what else to do while waiting for his brother to arrive, Ray prowls the house, discovering a will propped next to an antique Underwood typewriter. According to it, Ray and Forrest are his father's sole heirs, with property—what little there apparently is—to be divided equally between them.

But Ray's prowling doesn't stop there. He also discovers, much to his surprise, 27 boxes stuffed with $100 bills, totaling at least a couple million dollars. Where has this money come from, Ray wonders, and what should be done with it? When Forrest arrives, late, to the appointment with his father, Ray does not tell him about the cash. He fears that if Forrest had money, he would kill himself spending it in unhealthy ways.

Soon, Judge Reuben V. Atlee lies in state in the county courthouse, while Ray secretly transfers the boxes of cash from his father's house to the trunk of his Audi. Before he does anything else with it, however, he tries to determine whether his father's old friend and personal attorney, Harry Rex Varner, knows about the mysterious fortune. After a few visits, Ray concludes that Harry Rex is in the dark. Thus, following his father's funeral, Ray drives out of town and rents a room at one of the new motels in the area. He pays $39.99 for a double, carts in the sacks of money, and carefully, slowly counts what's there: $3,118,000.

First, he must determine whether the money is real. He knows he can't just take a few bills to the local bank and ask because doing so would stir up controversy. His solution is to bet with some of the bills at one of the nearby casinos. Casino employees, he reasons, are experts at spotting counterfeit money. Taking five $100 bills from different stacks of cash, Ray heads into the Santa Fe Club casino, one of the newer casinos in the area, and starts betting. Over the next several hours, he wins big. Because no one challenges him, Ray concludes the money may well be real. In fact, Ray wonders whether gambling could be the source of his father's windfall. But how to know for sure? And if it is, what should he do? Slowly, Ray realizes he is nearly as interested in protecting his father's reputation an in determining the source of the possibly ill-gotten gains.

Enter Claudia Gates, Ray's father's mistress and close friend. She arrives at the house the next day, right after Ray realizes the place was ransacked while he was away. As he did with Harry Rex, Ray tests Claudia to see if she knows about the money. She, too, seems clueless. In fact, she appears more interested in earning Ray's forgiveness than in driving a bargain about inheritance. Despite himself, Ray softens during their visit. When Claudia pronounces his father, the great man, a "sumbitch," they both laugh and agree (99).

Back home in Virginia, Ray works into the night getting the money from the trunk of his car into his house. The next morning, a call from Harry Rex awakens Ray at 9:00 A.M. Along with news that he has already hired a realtor and a cleaning service for the Clanton place comes word that Forrest has called to complain about his brother serving as executor of the estate. "Dad always liked him best" is the familiar version of Forrest's complaint. Because Forrest sounded drunk or high at the time of the call, Harry Rex and Ray decide not to worry too much about what he'll do.

On the Friday following his return from Clanton, Ray receives a package of sympathy mail Harry Rex has collected at the post office. In the stack is a pink envelope, inside of which is a card. The front reads, "With sympathy." Inside, however, are these words: "It would be a mistake to spend the money. The IRS is a phone call away" (150). Ray, who thought he'd gotten the money out of Clanton without anybody being the wiser, suddenly feels exposed. Someone knows about the cash he has taken, and depending on who that person is, it may be that neither Ray nor the fortune is safe.

Ray tightens security. He moves the money out of a storage unit with his name on it to one he rents in the name of NDY Ventures. A week or so later, pretending he is doing academic research, he travels to Washington,

D.C., to visit with someone at the Office of Printing and Engraving. An employee there gives Ray and readers a lesson in money illegalities. Identifying counterfeiting as a serious problem, he says the Treasury works hard to keep ahead of the bad guys using "printers that [give] the bills an almost holographic effect, watermarks, color-shifting inks, fine-line printing patterns, enlarged off-center portraits, and scanners that [can] spot a fake in less than an instant" (167).

Ray asks a pointed question. Could a person submit bills for testing? Yes, the employee answers, but if the bills are counterfeit, the person would lose them. That testing method closed to him, Ray speculates some more about how the money came to be in Judge Atlee's possession. He considers the possibility that his father may have taken bribes from lawyers wanting their cases heard earlier than was scheduled. But that explanation doesn't seem reasonable given the size of his father's docket, comparatively small, and the number of years his father served as a judge. In short, there is more money than Judge Atlee could possibly have accumulated during his time on the bench. Besides, his father had a reputation for scrupulous honesty, a reputation he had preserved over several decades.

Soon, Forrest shows up asking Ray for help. He is on the run from thugs, drug dealers whom he owes a considerable amount of money. Will Ray help him get into rehabilitation? Ray says yes and drives his brother to a nearby treatment center, Alcorn Village. Ray also signs the forms as guarantor of payment, even though Forrest whines that the money—a minimum of $9100—can be taken out of his inheritance.

Back in Clanton, Ray begins sifting through the judge's papers in search of other explanations for the money. Because, via Claudia, Harry Rex, and employees at the casino, Ray has all but ruled out gambling and graft, the next most likely explanation for the judge's riches rests with cases he heard as chancellor, or substitute judge, following his retirement from the bench. Hours into his research, Ray hits pay dirt: a zoning case on the Gulf Coast for which, mysteriously, there is no trial file. Ray is soon in coastal Mississippi, seeking more information about the trial his father conducted there.

At the courthouse in Bay St. Louis, Ray learns about the *Gibson v. Miyer-Brack* case. According to records, Clete Gibson is dead because of a cholesterol-lowering drug manufactured by Miyer-Brack. Although the drug Clete took lowered his cholesterol, it also destroyed his kidneys. Leading the case for the dead man before Chancellor Reuben V. Atlee was Patton French, attorney-at-law. Ray locates details of the case by visiting the Hancock County Courthouse and reading the pleadings, the discovery, and the trial transcript. These materials satisfy him that a conversation with French might offer up interesting information.

In a preliminary phone call, Ray gets what he expects from Patton French. French is, as Ray puts it, "a shameless ego pit" (253). Ray meets with him on board the *King of Torts,* French's luxury yacht anchored in the Gulf of Mexico. There Ray learns about his history as a pharmaceuticals litigator, about the cases he missed out on, and about those that made him rich. Ray also learns that French is the source of the mysterious $3 million now in Ray's possession. French had it delivered to Judge Atlee, without so much as a thank you card. It was sent in misguided fulfillment of a code that requires taking care of friends who have taken care of you. Judge Atlee was too ill to return the money, Ray guesses, and so Ray found it in boxes in the judge's study after his death.

French also reveals who is probably after the money: the man he asked to deliver it, the only person besides Ray and French who knew the money was there. That man is Gordie Priest, a small-time sleaze, whose brothers often work as his accomplices. French tells Ray to keep the cash, and he promises that efforts are being made to find Priest and "correct the problem." This is more information than Ray wants to know. As a parting gift, French gives Ray photos of the Priest boys so that he'll know who's looking for him. At this point, however, Ray has already endured numerous threats—he feels that he must return the money, or else.

The rest of *The Summons* describes Ray's efforts to hang on to the cash as well as others' actions designed to reclaim it. Depending on how sharp readers are, they may or may not be able to predict the twist in *The Summons*'s ending.

CHARACTER DEVELOPMENT

Ray Atlee

Like classical heroes, Ray Atlee is a loner with few friends or family members. He and his father have never been close, a fact Ray blames on his father's workaholism and neglect of him as a child. Ray's mother died when he was quite young, and he harbors many forms of resentment associated with her death. Ray's brother, Forrest, suffering from multiple addictions, is too involved with drugs to be a companion to anyone.

Heightening his solitary situation, Ray is recently divorced and feels acrimonious toward his former wife. He seems not to quite "get" why their marriage failed. According to him, one day she simply walked out of their house and married a local wealthy, but shady, business tycoon, known around town as Lew the Liquidator. Ray is deeply pained by his wife's desertion and by the fact she is pregnant with Lew's child.

Rather than looking for a new partner himself, Ray develops a hobby, flying, which, sadly, further isolates him. Lonely and alienated, Ray allows his anger toward his former wife to fester. He makes clear that one reason he has chosen flying as a pastime is that aviation provides cheaper therapy than does time spent with a psychologist. Money is a big issue for Ray. Lack of it kept him out of Stanford, where he'd been admitted as a college freshman. Lack of it, he thinks, may have caused his former wife to desert him for a wealthier man.

But as is also the case with classical heroes, Ray possesses many positive qualities as well. He is smart and courageous, deftly responding to his father's summons and wisely protecting the money he finds stashed in his father's home. But is he honest? It is difficult to be sure, especially because he doesn't immediately tell Forrest about the boxes of money to which Forrest might be as entitled as Ray is.

Ray appears, in fact, to be one of Grisham's loneliest and saddest protagonists. Most Grisham heroes have a spouse, friend, confidante, or colleague with whom they are close. Ray has only his *father's* best friend to drink with and a female student, back home in Virginia, who wants a closer relationship with Ray than he does with her. Like many of Grisham's male protagonists, Ray appears to have intimacy problems, especially where women are concerned. It's hard not to feel sorry for him as he drives back and forth between Virginia and Mississippi, lacking even a friend to call from the road.

One gets the feeling though that Grisham *wants* readers to care about Ray ("Why else would he have Ray's gold-digging wife leave him for a pudgy local millionaire?" wonders reviewer Benjamin Svetkey). After all, there's nothing criminal about Grisham's protagonist, and he isn't mean. He still cares for his ex-wife, despite her grievous behavior toward him, and he even "brushes off advances from beautiful young law students because sleeping with them would be inappropriate" (Svetkey).

Still, there are puzzling issues that surround the protagonist of *The Summons*. Readers may wonder whether Ray Atlee is heroic at all. He seems only vaguely interested in seeking self-knowledge through his adventures with the mysterious cash, and he doesn't seem at all committed to helping others. He barely mourns never having reconciled with his father, nor does he seem particularly conflicted about hiding money from his brother. Instead, Ray expends his energies figuring out whether, and if so how, he can keep the cash, causing one reviewer to conclude he is "uninteresting except when he is unlikable" (Liptak) and another that Ray is "repellently self-centered and materialistic" (Dugdale).

Secondary Characters

Other than Ray, there are no characters in *The Summons* whom Grisham develops in any detail. Both key secondary characters, Ray's brother Forrest and Harry Rex, his father's best friend, are flat: Forrest is a caricature of a drug addict, and Harry Rex is the quintessential southern buddy and drinking companion. In fact, the most interesting of secondary characters is Judge Reuben Atlee, the dead man himself, who, we are told, is well respected and even loved by the community, if not by his sons.

Given that Grisham had just finished *A Painted House* and *Skipping Christmas,* the fact that he didn't create fully developed characters in *The Summons* seems surprising. Grisham easily shows in both of his non-thrillers that he is capable of carving out at least *rounded* characters if not round ones. Here *no one* is round. In fact, as one critic wrote, "money [flat bills] is the most engaging character in the book" (Liptak).

PLOT DEVELOPMENT

The Summons is structured circularly, its introductory paragraph neatly hinting at the secrets in the novel's conclusion. Opening sentences focus on the letter calling Ray and Forrest to Clanton—the summons itself—and on Judge Atlee's fascination with Civil War hero Nathan Bedford Forrest, after whom the judge named his younger son.

One of the pleasures of a Grisham plot is that readers usually learn a lot about peculiar subjects: how to conceal money by wiring it to various banks in the Caribbean, for example, or how to stay one step ahead in a chase. In *The Summons,* Grisham has plenty of interest to say about counterfeit money—how to make it and how to trace it—and about casino operations, class-action suits, rehabilitation centers, and types of airplanes. Such facts by themselves can often be an effective tool for sustaining reader interest, and they perform their job admirably in *The Summons.*

Otherwise, Grisham uses at least two devices in this, his fourteenth novel, to keep readers riveted to the action. First, he introduces an intriguing question or piece of information at the end of several chapters, implicitly promising an answer in the chapter to come ("And why hide it [the money]? Why not give it away like the rest of his money?" [90]). Second, he summarizes frequently so that readers whose attention has wandered are drawn gently back into the plot ("Through the blur of the last four days, he had concentrated only on getting the money to the spot where it was now located. Now he had to plan the next step and he had very few ideas" [137]).

The story Grisham retells in *The Summons* is an old one: that money is at the root of evil or that "money corrupts big time" (Millar). That said, Grisham contemporizes it in an interesting way. Readers who enjoy travel are especially likely to be hooked by the plot. Ray Atlee spends much of the novel in his car, motoring first between Virginia and Mississippi and then making a side trip to Alabama, to question the super-rich class-action attorney Patton French.

Similarly, readers fascinated by aviation will also enjoy this novel. In recent years, Grisham has evidently learned how to fly, an interest he ascribes to his protagonist in *The Summons* as well. Ray flies places as often as he drives, graduating from Cessnas to larger and cushier Bonanzas after discovering the money at his father's house.

As usual, reviewers praised Grisham's "surefire" plotting above all else in *The Summons* (Anderson). They lauded his "knack for jump-starting a story"; his ability to hook readers with "an instant mystery . . . something universal . . . in this case . . . the fear of losing a parent with too much left resolved"; his "powerfully familiar and sympathetic characters"; and his "clean, forthright, propulsive style" (Maslin).

Although strong stories have a way of "collapsing after . . . initial clever plotting runs out," that doesn't happen here (Maslin). Grisham avoids "bogus suspects, breathless violent action with the hero on the run and a boring romance with a generically flirty, available woman." Instead, he "keeps a lid on such things and sustains his book's tight focus" (Maslin).

The few critics with complaints about plot have said that Grisham isn't as successful as usual in pulling together the story's disparate threads. Although "it's nice that, in the last few pages, there isn't a tidy conclusion . . . there's [also] never a sense that a powerful story has marched toward a proper resolution" (Guinn).

Another frequent complaint, this one with considerable merit, is that the plot of *The Summons* contains numerous implausibilities, more so than any previous Grisham novel. Why in the world would a father issue a written "summons" to sons he could have called? Why does Ray respond by driving 15 hours to Mississippi without phoning ahead or on the way? How could the slovenly Forrest stay at Judge Atlee's home for eight days before his father died and leave no traces of his presence there? Why does Ray reveal the money's location to a security guard he doesn't know? Why does he confide in his father's girlfriend, Claudia, whom at first he doesn't trust? Why does he try to buy her silence with $25,000 *after* he concludes she doesn't know about the money? Why does Ray talk so freely on cell phones without fearing his conversations are being overheard? And "why does a rapacious plaintiff's lawyer opt . . . to dispense with a jury for the biggest trial of his career[?] Having won it fair and square, [why does he] bribe . . . the incorruptible judge anyway?" (Liptak).

SETTING AND SOCIAL AND LITERARY CONTEXTS

Much of the novel's action takes place in Clanton, Mississippi, where Grisham's favorite first novel, *A Time to Kill*, is also set. Given that Grisham returns to Clanton in *The Summons* after 12 novels set elsewhere, one might expect setting to signal something significant, particularly in terms of social context or theme. This doesn't seem to be the case.

One explanation for *The Summons*'s setting might be that Grisham planned a series of novels that would take place in Clanton, *The Summons* serving as the second among them. *The King of Torts*, Grisham fifteenth novel, however, returns to Washington, D.C., and to torts attorney Patton French, negating this possibility, and there is nothing else in *The Summons* to suggest Grisham plans a sequel.

More likely, Grisham sought to contrast the Old and New South in the novel. Especially in early chapters, Grisham seems interested in comparing Judge Atlee, the embodiment of Old Southern values, with his two sons, neither of whom is connected to old ways. Grisham calls Judge Atlee's estate Maple Run, which Forrest quickly subverts to Maple Ruin.

Although Forrest is named after the Civil War hero Nathan Bedford Forrest, he hardly embodies the qualities of old-world Southern character that Bedford presumably does. Instead, Forrest and Ray, Grisham writes, are of a "bloodline [that] was thinning to a sad and inevitable halt" (7). Even the town of Clanton seems moribund. Of the Atlee neighborhood, Grisham writes, "The red and yellow maples that once lined the street had died of some unknown disease" (6). About the family home, he says, "It was still a handsome house, a Georgian with columns, once a monument to those who'd built it, and now a sad reminder of a declining family . . . filled with unpleasant memories" (7). And Judge Rueben Atlee does die at Maple "Ruin."

The Summons as Quest Novel

A central topic in literature of every culture, past and present, is the heroic quest, during which someone accustomed to a comfortable, mostly passive life is "called" to adventure and chooses to strive toward some important goal. Reluctantly accepting the call of responsibility, heroes cross "thresholds," entering worlds simultaneously dangerous and full of potential. In those worlds, questers are tested as they struggle to attain the prizes they seek.

Questers' searches in literature are as varied as the protagonists who make them. Setting out from stagnant communities, heroes eventually return home to revitalize or "redeem" the places they left behind, using the lessons of travel to do so. Examples of classic quest heroes include Oedipus, Sir Gawain, and assorted pilgrims in *The Canterbury Tales*. Modern writers, many of them American, have been especially interested in the quest theme. William Faulkner, Flannery O'Connor, F. Scott Fitzgerald, Stephen Crane, Bernard Malamud, Ernest Hemingway, and John Barth, to name just a few, have written literature featuring the quest.

The Summons could be described as both a legal thriller and a quest novel, detailing Ray Atlee's travels to figure out his moral and legal obligations to his father, brother, profession, and "society" at large. Certainly, the culture that Ray grew up in—the Old South of homey Clanton, Mississippi—can be characterized as passive and powerless. One of the obligations Ray shoulders includes deciding what to do with the money in his possession. Should he keep it, return it to whomever it belongs, share it with Forrest, or donate it to a worthy cause?

Most quest heroes are physically, morally, and emotionally strong, but have a single flaw, making them vulnerable to poor decision-making. Ray Atlee is physically strong (capable of toting all those money bags), but morally and emotionally awash. He lacks confidence that he knows what is right. Instead, he finds himself in a battle of wits against those who would take the money away from him.

Ray's travels metaphorically represent an internal journey toward figuring out what he should do with the money. On this journey, he must also struggle to resolve issues from a painful childhood. Although Grisham remains somewhat vague about the nature of those issues, readers learn that they involve parents and siblings, as most childhood problems do. The question implied but never explored is can Ray resolve what's troubling him, and in the process will he figure out how to do the right thing?

THEMES

Humans Cannot Escape Responsibilities to Each Other

Although Ray doesn't appear to struggle much with his conscience over hiding the $3 million, readers are encouraged to ponder what *they* would do if placed in similar circumstances. In effect, readers "quest" nearly as much as Ray does. Is it morally and ethically right to accept money under Ray's circumstances? After a windfall such as the one Ray experiences, what are one's obligations to others?

Money Is the Root of All Evil

Although money can represent greater freedom and more choices, it also can, as happens in *The Summons,* lead to further avarice. Certainly, Ray appears to lose track of his own values, if he ever had any, as he struggles to hang on to money that does not really belong to him. In the end, money seems not to have made Ray any happier than he was before he discovered it.

Modern America: A Lonely, Rootless, and Greedy Place

The world—the United States, the New South?—in which Ray operates is characterized as rootless, lonely, and obsessively greedy. Gone are people like Judge Reuben V. Atlee for whom, evidently, there may be more important possessions than cold, hard cash.

The Crucial Nature of Father–Son Relationships and the Complexity of Human Behavior

Grisham argues for the importance of the father–son relationship, but he also alludes to problems inherent in it. Human nature is complicated and contradictory. Ray's father is a case in point in that there appears to be a disjuncture between his public persona and his private life. Publicly, Judge Atlee is the embodiment of generosity and kindness. Eulogies praise a man who sent poor kids to college and choir children to New York competitions. On the other hand, both of his sons, to one degree or another, seem "ruined," at least in part because of their father's neglect.

Sibling Rivalry Can Lead to Great Emotional Pain

Sibling rivalry is a frequent theme in literature, dating back to biblical stories about jealousy between Cain and Abel, Jacob and Esau, and Joseph and his brothers. Ray and Forrest portray troubled sibling roles consistent with their birth order. Ray is the responsible first born who strives to be successful, but is incapable of feeling satisfied with anything he has accomplished. Forrest is the irresponsible, and some might say spoiled, younger sibling, whose excessive use of drugs and alcohol sadly embodies selfishness and a greed different from but related to Ray's.

CRITICAL RESPONSES

Despite some negative reactions to the novel, reviews of *The Summons* tend to be more positive than those of other recent Grisham works. Even critics who don't care for the novel have praised it, if faintly.

The novel's most positive reviews appeared in East Coast and large national newspapers: the *New York Times,* the *Washington Post,* and *USA Today.* The *New York Times* reviewer called *The Summons* "a successful . . . return . . . to form." This is a book of "highly salable simplicity," the reviewer added, grounded in "enough . . . reflective intelligence to give . . . [it] its ballast. Mr. Grisham seems genuinely interested in the questions of conscience that snare Ray, and he makes them matter" (Maslin). The *Washington Post* reviewer praised *The Summons* for being "a pleasure to read and, considered all in all, a model of what good commercial fiction can be." This reviewer, in fact, referred to Grisham's "exceptional skill as a storyteller on display in *The Summons.*" "Any editor," he added, "can toss out a recipe for a bestseller, but not one writer in 10,000 has the magic [as Grisham does in this novel] to cook up a seamless story with near-universal appeal" (Anderson). According to the reviewer for *USA Today,* *The Summons* "ranks as my absolute favorite in many years." As to reasons for liking the novel, she counted them:

> First, there is an ending too delicious and morally instructive to give away. Second, the novel . . . skillfully tours the New South of gambling casinos, endless self-storage centers and ultra-rich lawyers who sue multinational corporations. Third, *The Summons* turns the mirror on the readers' own assumptions about other human beings, including the very flawed. To wheel out the old cliché, I gobbled this book down in one sitting, not for work but for pleasure. (Donahue)

Less favorable reviews mention the novel's positive elements, but emphasize its negative ones. For the *Boston Globe,* Richard Dyer wrote that *The Summons* is "full of promising raw material," but he criticized Grisham for turning out "a lazy, shoddy book that might as well be called *The Formula.*" Another reviewer, this one for *Entertainment Weekly,* wrote that *The Summons* is "not necessarily a bad book—indeed, in some ways Grisham has never been a better-behaved writer—but ultimately it's a mystery in which the most shocking surprise turns out to be how few shocking surprises there are in it" (Svetkey). The *Times* of London called *The Summons* "classic Grisham: a mundane moral fable of moderately diverting and undemanding prose" (Millar). London's *Sunday Telegraph* described the novel as "an intriguing failure rather than a fully achieved success" (Spencer), with a reviewer in the *Sunday Times* deeming it a "social satire that never quite coheres" (Dugdale).

9

The King of Torts
(2003)

John Grisham notes that occasionally he comes up with an idea for his next book while writing another one. This anticipatory creativity apparently occurred while he was writing *The Summons*. A key character in it wanders into Grisham's fifteenth novel, *The King of Torts*. In *The Summons*, Patton French, an attorney who does mass tort litigation—suing a company or individual on behalf of a large group of complainants—slips Judge Reuben Atlee $3 million for getting his clients a good verdict in a pharmaceuticals case. In *The King of Torts*, French plays a more prominent role, as does the topic of mass tort litigation. The companies that do wrong, their consumer victims, and the evils of class-action lawsuits constitute Grisham's cause célèbre this time around.

That said, there must have been prepublication uneasiness surrounding the book's title, with someone, maybe the writer himself, worried whether readers would know "a *tort* from a *tart*" (Guinn). And whoever was doing the hand-wringing must have won out because the book's dust jacket features a printed definition of *tort*, excerpted from *Black's Law Dictionary:*

> Tort (from Lat. *torquere,* to twist, *tortus*, twisted, wrested aside).
> A private or civil wrong or injury, including action for bad
> faith or breach of contract, for which the court will provide a
> remedy in the form of an action for damages.

Grisham's treatment of mass tort litigation is certainly timely. Few adults today are wholly ignorant of tort cases and large-scale tort litigations. Television and bulk mailings to potential litigants who have purchased faulty batteries, defective computer accessories, or flawed insurance policies ensure that many Americans wrongly believe they are mere days away from a huge settlement in a class-action lawsuit. For that reason, *The King of Torts* seems to have touched a nerve, ensuring another Grisham novel its usual few million readers. In fact, it ended 2003 ranked third among best-selling hardcover books, behind Dan Brown's *The Da Vinci Code* and Mitch Albom's *The Five People You Meet in Heaven*.

Although *The King of Torts* is not his favorite work (that ranking is reserved for *A Painted House*), Grisham likes its message. The novel is, he says, "an exploration of class action lawsuits and the vast sums of money that lawyers are making off them that they really don't deserve." Although Grisham admits "the plot was a little farfetched," he wants readers to know that such scams "really do . . . happen" (*Entertainment Weekly*).

PLOT

Grisham's Faustian tale begins as many of his thrillers do, with violence: five gunshots into the head of a young man from the streets of Washington, D.C., someone nicknamed Pumpkin. Pumpkin's real name is Ramon Pumphrey; he is young, poor, black, and drug-addicted. The perpetrator is Tequila Watson, age 20, also poor and black, and like Pumpkin, he has a history of drug addiction. Tequila is quickly caught and jailed, but he soon claims he has no idea why he committed the murder.

The protagonist of *The King of Torts* is par for Grisham. A young attorney, age 31, and something of a loner, his name is Jarrett Clay Carter II. His parents are divorced, and his father, an ex-lawyer himself, now lives a bohemian life in the Caribbean. Clay has been a public defender for nearly five years. Stopping past the D.C. Superior Court Criminal Division, Felony Branch, to check on clients, Clay is fully visible when the judge looks around the courtroom for someone to defend Tequila.

But there is another key character. A stranger sharing an elevator with Clay—as Mister did with attorney Michael Brock in *The Street Lawyer*—shows up right at the end of chapter 1. "A fortyish gentleman dressed in designer black—jeans, T-shirt, jacket, alligator boots"—he stares at Clay, who doesn't see the man in black watching him (7).

Over the next several chapters, this man disappears while readers learn more about Clay, about the workings of the Office of the Public Defender,

and about Clay's early efforts on behalf of Tequila. Like most Grisham protagonists, Clay is involved in a bad relationship with a woman. Although
unmarried, Clay has a longtime girlfriend, Rebecca Van Horn, whose
ultraconservative, materialistic parents he doesn't care for (the father is an
unscrupulous real estate developer). For that matter, he has doubts about
Rebecca herself, a staffer for a low-ranking congressional representative.
Soon, she has broken up with him because, according to her, he has no
ambition and no future.

A few days pass, and Clay is sipping his morning coffee and reading
the sports page when the phone rings. At first, he thinks Rebecca wants
him back; she's the only person who'd be likely to call at 7:20 A.M. Instead,
the caller identifies himself as Max Pace, a headhunter who wants to talk
with Clay about jobs with a couple of law firms. He is also, readers be
forewarned, the "man in black" on the elevator. Dazzled by opportunity,
Clay sets an appointment with him.

They meet at noon at the Willard Intercontinental Hotel. A man who is
plainly a bodyguard escorts Clay upstairs to Pace's room. Quickly, Clay
realizes the situation is not what it seems. Why wouldn't a headhunter
talk with him downstairs in a hotel restaurant? Why would a headhunter
have a bodyguard?

Max Pace explains that he works for a company hired by other companies to clean up legal messes. So begins Pace's tale about a drug, Tarvan,
which is supposed to cure addiction to "opium- and cocaine-based nar-
cotics" (68). Rushing to get their drug on the market and profits rolling in,
the company didn't run proper tests before releasing it. Afterward, they
performed minimal testing, which confirmed that Tarvan cures addictions, but also that, sadly, in 8 percent of cases, it makes people kill, "plain
and simple" (70). By the time the drug company realized Tarvan's flaw,
five people in the D.C. area had been murdered by those taking it (Pumpkin being one of them), and a sixth was in a coma.

Max gets to the point: the firm he represents wants Clay to make
repairs by compensating families of the Washington victims, securing
four-million-dollar settlements for each. For his work, Max will pay Clay
$10 million. The offer shocks the modestly paid public defender. Clay
wanders the streets of central Washington, D.C., pondering Max's offer.
He will be able to help the families of the victims, but what about people
like Tequila, who, in their own ways, are victims too? Max has said there's
nothing to be done for them. They are killers and might as well be dead.
Despite misgivings based on years as a public defender and after a dis-
appointing trip to the Bahamas to consult with his alcoholic ex-attorney

father, Clay accepts Pace's offer, negotiating a higher fee for himself—$15 million—and $5 million for each of his clients-to-be. A friend, Rodney, from the public defender's office joins Clay's fledgling firm.

The process of paying off Tarvan's victims gets underway. Rodney talks to Pumpkin's mother at work, using file material on the case prepared by Max Pace. Clay drives to West Virginia to work with the parents of a young man shot outside a Starbucks. A search for the family of a third victim, Bandy, a prostitute, is unsuccessful. The last family members of a victim to sign are the parents of a 20-year-old Howard University dropout. Although at first they're resistant, they eventually add their names to papers agreeing to a settlement. Clay, meanwhile, can now afford to buy himself a black Porsche and a house on a quiet Georgetown street. Although he worries about values—is he spending too much money? Is he spending it in proper ways?—He justifies these two expenses. He *could*, he reasons, be a lot more lavish.

Max is soon back in conversations with Clay about another case, this one involving an anti-arthritic drug called Dyloft, said to cause bladder tumors in users. Max represents a company in competition with Dyloft's manufacturers—Ackerman Labs—who wish to curtail Ackerman's successes by suing them.

Suing will be easy. All they need to do is locate enough clients and, through urinalysis, identify probable tumor cases. Research has shown that the tumors are benign, so the problem can be corrected by a simple cystiscopical procedure. Nobody gets hurt, Clay rationalizes, and he will become even richer.

So that Clay can learn more about mass litigation, Max Pace suggests he attend a conference in New Orleans. The Circle of Barristers meet there annually to discuss large-scale torts and the "latest trends in litigation" (124). Clay is shocked by what he sees at the group's meetings: a feeding frenzy of consumerism. Law is barely a focus. Instead, manufacturers of airplanes and yachts and luxury cars are there to sell their products to lawyers made rich by large-scale class-action suits. People with Caribbean real estate and Montana cattle ranches to peddle are there too. While in New Orleans, Clay receives a bitter blow. A staffer faxes him Rebecca's engagement announcement from the Washington newspapers. Not even a month has gone by since her breakup with Clay, and she is engaged to a rich and successful young D.C. attorney. Clay reels from the wounding.

Back in Washington, Clay's tort practice continues to grow. Astoundingly wealthy torts attorney Patton French courts Clay, suggesting they merge their Dyloft efforts. French holds a team kick-off meeting at his ranch in Ketchum, Idaho. Clay charters a Learjet to attend and enjoys watching other lawyers posturing for each other, all the while holding himself above the herd. Soon, however, he is getting in trouble financially by "illegally speculating on the stocks his [own] lawsuits are about to ruin" (Appelo).

He also calls Rebecca to urge her not to marry her fiancé, but she hangs up on him. In a retaliatory effort, he asks a friend to set him up with a good-looking female to take, uninvited, to Rebecca's wedding. "I need a bimbo," he tells the friend, "preferably a blonde" (214). The woman he is set up with goes by a single name, Ridley. She is a model from the former Soviet state of Georgia, and she and Clay have little in common (her interests are shopping and old movies).

As these details and his increasingly dangerous behavior show, Clay Carter is spinning out of control. Even if he wanted to, he can't stop doing mass litigation because he has huge overhead expenses to meet. Besides, hubris keeps him out of check. Soon he is filing a lawsuit against Hannah Portland Cement, in Reedsburg, Pennsylvania, a company that has sold mortar that "flakes away between the bricks" (Dyer). Hannah admits it is at fault, but Clay goes after the company anyway. It's a case that may ruin the cement company and may also lead to Clay's downfall. Readers wonder how Grisham can possibly rescue his protagonist, mired so deeply in a self-created bog.

CHARACTER DEVELOPMENT

Jarrett Clay Carter II

Like several Grisham protagonists, Clay Carter (he has dropped the Jarrett, his father's name) shares much in common with the classical tragic hero whom Aristotle describes in *The Poetics*. Because of a flaw or *hamartia*, this hero suffers a downfall. Clay's flaw is double: he is both prideful and greedy. As a result of these defects, his descent is sure to be painful. Readers are propelled forward in the narrative, wondering whether Clay will also eventually experience illumination and redemption.

Some reviews draw parallels between Clay in *The King of Torts* and the great Renaissance tragic figure, Doctor Faustus. In fact, *The King of Torts* is arguably a contemporary, popularized retelling of Christopher Marlowe's *The Tragicall History of the Life and Death of Doctor Faustus*, the early seventeenth-century English tragedy set in Germany and Italy. Dr. Faustus sells his soul to Lucifer, via Mephistopheles, in exchange for 24 years of extraordinary power. Clay Carter sells his to Mammon, via Max Pace, for the same reason. Clay feels he has good reason to do so. His credentials (a law degree from Georgetown) suggest he could do far better than the job he holds in the public defender's office and a salary in the $40,000 bracket. Besides he has just lost a girlfriend because, presumably, her parents think he lacks prospects.

Like Faustus, Clay is ambitious and intelligent, in the beginning using these qualities for the greater public good. When Clay's girlfriend dumps him, in part because he refuses to work for her father, anger blinds him. His subsequent rise to power and wealth is so swift and steep that there's little wonder why Clay refuses to see the truth himself or listen to those who warn him about the impropriety, not to mention illegality, of his behavior.

Faustus is a sympathetic character in that he travels the world seeking knowledge; Clay's motivations are shallower. He skips around the United States and assorted Caribbean Islands in search of more and still more money and—a truth only gradually revealed—in search of approval from his father. Still, even when he is earning $110 million a year, he feels little satisfaction other than what he can accrue through shallow gloating.

Thus, after he sells his soul to the devilish Max Pace, he comes across to some readers as unmitigated "scum" (Dyer). Even so, others can still relate to Clay, perhaps because Grisham incites in them the "pity" and "fear" Aristotle mentions in *The Poetics* as "cathartic emotions." Besides, given materialist values in present-day United States, it is difficult *not* to identify with Clay's glee as he accrues still more wealth.

One criticism leveled at characterization in *The King of Torts* is that Grisham fails to give Clay an "inner life" and never really explores why Clay sells out. Although there may be some validity in this point, staying on the surface is part of Grisham's art. Reviewers tend to criticize characterization in a Grisham novel while praising its pacing, ignoring the fact that pacing results as much from what is left out as from what is put in. As one critic put it, "Sustaining momentum, not building character, is Grisham's specialty" (Kirschling).

Even so, Grisham might have done something to justify Clay's metamorphosis from an all right guy into a thoughtless scoundrel, a greedy jerk, "a strange person" for readers "to be asked to root for" (Kirschling). In the end of *Doctor Faustus*, Faust repents, crying out, "I'll burn my books!" Clay Carter isn't properly sorry, merely longing for "two good legs and a clean slate" while still enjoying the last trappings of wealth, an overseas flight in his personal jet (372).

Max Pace

Dressed in black right down to his alligator boots, Grisham's Mephistopheles, Max Pace, looks as much like country singer Johnny Cash as the devil. Although Marlowe's Mephistopheles is an interestingly ambivalent character similar to John Milton's Satan in *Paradise Lost*, Max Pace is flat and unremittingly evil, continuing to offer Clay more work and, thereby, feeding his greed.

Max's role in *The King of Torts* resembles that of Teddy Maynard in *The Brethren*. Both lurk in the background as evil puppeteers pulling the strings.

Patton French

Of the secondary characters, Patton French is the most interestingly depicted. He is one of the few characters "too colorful to be drawn in moral black or white." In fact, French "serves nicely as the book's [moral] barometer. Once Clay starts doing things that even this guy won't touch, it's time for the downhill slide" (Maslin).

Female Characters

Female characters in *The King of Torts* are particularly "one-dimensional" and, as such, unbelievable (Maslin). Clay is out of contact with his own mother, and his girlfriend's mother is viciously mercenary. The girlfriend, Rebecca, is "only faintly ambiguous: she drives an evil German sports car, but still likes to have sex with Clay five times a week" (Maslin). That she marries someone so quickly after breaking up with Clay does not say much that's good about her character. That she soon divorces this man because he works too hard "doesn't ring true" (Dyer). As for the "bimbo" girlfriend, Ridley, she is consummately vain and materialistic. Like Patton French, she serves as a tidy comparison to Rebecca, making the selfish latter look less offensive.

Other Secondary Characters

As usual, other secondary characters are flat, sent from "central casting." Most are mass tort lawyers and "universally unlikable" (Brett).

PLOT DEVELOPMENT

The King of Torts falls into two parts. Chapters 1–7 portray Clay's life as a public defender up to his painful breakup with Rebecca. Chapters 8–42 tell the rest of the story, focusing on Clay's new life as a mass torts attorney. The two sections are only tangentially related, in that the drug Tarvan, which is the focus of Clay's first torts case in part 2, causes Tequila to murder Pumpkin in part 1. After Clay compensates Pumpkin's family for his untimely death, readers hear little about either Tequila or Pumpkin again. The direction in which the plot heads beginning with chapter 8 is toward the subplot of *The Summons*. Patton French, the torts attorney who pays off Reuben Atlee in *The Summons*, reappears, and along with him comes a host of other such attorneys with whom Clay Carter greedily plots to garner megabuck profits.

Grisham has a huge task in shaping plot in *The King of Torts*. Not only must he tell an engaging story, but he must also make some fairly complex legal terms and processes understandable to his readers. That, of course, is part of his art, and Grisham performs admirably. Still, the novel tends to have less physical action and intrigue than his earlier books, even less than the bucolic non-thriller *A Painted House*: fewer car chases, mysterious break-ins, and other types of overt intimidation (Singhania). Its "narrative arc" predictable, *The King of Torts* contains hardly any of the breath-holding excitement of, say, *The Firm*'s characters trying to uncover evidence in the Grand Caymans or, in *The Pelican Brief*, of Darby Shaw on the lam around New Orleans, New York, and Washington, D.C. (Dugdale). There is a murder at the novel's beginning and an assault toward the end. The plot of *The King of Torts* also offers virtually no courtroom scenes, Grisham focusing instead on Clay's out-of-court maneuverings.

As with other Grisham books, this one is packed full of information; however, there is disagreement about the value of the data presented. Several critics have claimed that readers are exposed to "loads of one-dimensional facts" about mass torts and other topics, but that the pieces of information "fool . . . [people] into thinking they're learning something" (Guinn). Those who see value in what Grisham presents have made the stronger argument. Certainly, readers come away from *The King of Torts* with a clearer understanding of class-action lawsuits, grist to use in pondering the moral and ethical issues attendant to them.

There is also controversy about Grisham's attitude toward some of the fancy "adult toys"—yachts, airplanes, fancy homes—he describes, a few critics believing Grisham is obsessively interested in these objects. In fact, there *does* seem to be a fairly high degree of "voyeurism" in the novel. Although he condemns greed and corruption, Grisham seems to spend more time describing "the wonders of the Gulfstream jet than the book's tsk-tsking really requires" (Maslin).

All things considered, however, Grisham's plotting in *The King of Torts* continues to fascinate, one critic comparing Grisham to "a kid playing with blocks. He spends the first two thirds of the book building Clay's kingdom. Then he begins pulling out a few blocks so the whole structure begins to sway before it topples" (Pate). Although some reviewers disapproved of the radical shift in direction the novel takes on "page 67" (Dyer), complained about "preachy dialogue" (Guinn), carped that the novel is not as "atmospheric" as usual (Donahue), and claimed it contains too much "formula writing" (Cogdill), each of these criticisms is made respectfully and with plenty of countering praise. Overall, Grisham continues to be thought of as the "master of plot and pacing" (Guinn), a man with "a sterling gift for storytelling" (Kirschling).

SOCIAL AND LITERARY CONTEXTS

The King of Torts deals with a key issue in the United States today, mass torts abuse. A litigious culture, we sue one another and those who provide us with products and services at the drop of a faulty purchase or small accident. Mass tort litigation makes it possible for individuals who would never think of suing over a malfunctioning can opener or the way we are billed by credit card companies to get satisfaction as a group, whereas, alone, we would rarely find litigation worth the time or money. Suddenly, an ad appears on television or a card arrives in the mail inviting us to join thousands of others who feel similarly mistreated. There is, of course, the lure of a huge settlement, but the print is so small and the language of the advertisement is so lawyerly that potential plaintiffs can't really see that lawyers are profiting far more than consumers do. Grisham apparently feels that the lawyers who get rich off of such suits are more evil than the corporations who make the faulty products or offer faulty services (Anderson).

At least one critic sees *The King of Torts* as a "propaganda victory for the White House, the corporations, the insurance companies and all those who want to see legislation that caps jury verdicts and otherwise discourages class actions." As he put it, "One of the few issues that clearly divide Democrats and Republicans these days is the former's willingness to support the trial lawyers (their great contributors) and the latter's eagerness to defend the corporations (their great contributors) against the horrors of class-action cases." He feels Grisham's novel would have been better had it been more evenhanded, presenting both sides of this "complex issue" (Anderson). Another critic objected to Grisham's "preaching from the bully pulpit of best-sellerdom," adding, "if only [the book's] characters were as lively as its indignation" (Maslin). But then one wonders where else a man like Grisham might better preach.

THEMATIC ISSUES

The King of Torts is a fable, a morality or cautionary tale, and as such, it explores numerous thematic threads. It shares some themes in common with Marlowe's tragedy *Dr. Faustus.* Christopher Marlowe, writing in the seventeenth century, heavy-handedly preaches, and even Grisham, whose theater of operation is a contemporary world, does a fair amount of sermonizing.

The Dangers of Pride

Grisham's *The King of Torts* is a secular story, but it nevertheless confirms that pride, one of Christianity's "Seven Deadly Sins," causes Clay Carter's ironic fall from hardworking public defense attorney to wildly successful torts lawyer. Pride leads to greed and a legion of other sins. Chief among them is extraordinary selfishness. As one who has looked out for the welfare of the poor since graduating from law school, Clay transforms all too quickly into a lowlife shyster.

The Desire for Power Leads to Corruption

Although Faustus wants power that is attendant to both money *and* knowledge, Clay's drive is a single, simple one: to make as much cash as he can as quickly as possible. Great wealth enables him to acquire a condominium in the Caribbean and a flashy airplane as well as a vapid beauty, Ridley, to adorn his acquisitions. It does not, however, provide him with happiness, nor does it enable him to live a better life according to any standard other than strictly monetary.

Good versus Evil: The Two Contradictory Voices That Speak to Us

Like Dr. Faustus, Clay Carter periodically considers whether he is doing the right thing, but unlike Faustus, he doesn't worry a lot. Even though opposing interior voices periodically whisper to him, Clay single-mindedly travels on a greedy self-destructive path.

In *Dr. Faustus,* the voices of conscience are embodied as good and evil angels. In *The King of Torts,* Clay's contradictory impulses are described in more worldly fashion. Although Clay "struggles occasionally to make the right choice, there is little doubt he will let us down and succumb to what turns out to be a big, bad corporate conspiracy. In the end, [however] idealism, or some form of it, survives intact" (Singhania).

The Evils of Greed

Although there is overlap between power and greed in both *Dr. Faustus* and the *King of Torts,* Grisham distinguishes between them. He doesn't object to power so much as he despises its misuse. After all, many of Grisham's heroes, including Clay Carter, start from a base of power (they are, after all, mostly male, comfortably middle-class, and relatively well-off attorneys). Grisham is clear in *The King of Torts* that the greater sin is greed, taking more than one can well use. Grisham makes a similar point in *The Summons* and elsewhere, but nowhere does he state this message more clearly or more powerfully than in *The King of Torts.* Here Clay's mass tort attorney colleagues embody excess and self-interest, Grisham "effectively detail[ing] all the accoutrements of modern success, from the Porsche to the model girlfriend to the jet" (Donahue). Eventually, Grisham believes, we pay for our avarice. As one reviewer wrote, "Grisham believes in the fictional 'karma' of sinners reaping what they sow. Anyone who's read even one of the author's previous legal-themed thrillers will anticipate the eventual outcome, if not the means by which Clay's tort kingdom is brought down" (Guinn). Whatever the result in *The King of Torts,* Grisham develops this theme so powerfully that readers can't help wondering what they themselves would do for 15 million dollars (Donahue).

The Value of Friendship

It is worth noting that Clay's friends in the Office of the Public Defender remain true supporters throughout his rise and fall. Rebecca, too, in her fashion remains connected to him despite the marital alliance her parents encourage her to make. As the *Washington Post* reviewer correctly noted, "Grisham wants to show us that love conquers all, but he writes far less persuasively about women than he does about tort law and Gulfstream jets" (Anderson).

CRITICAL REVIEWS

The King of Torts earned many more positive than negative reviews. Those who like the novel have generally praised Grisham for being "timely" and for his clear moral voice (Pate). One critic at first seemed snide, labeling Grisham "the poster boy for simplistic presentation and equally simplistic moralizing." He added, however, "That's not necessarily criticism. In any art form, particularly fiction, the key to 2003 sales success is entertainment. Grisham's readers want to feel like they're learning a lot without having to think especially hard. *The King of Torts* . . . fills that bill" (Guinn). Another's praise was less qualified: "*The King of Torts* scores points for providing an inside glimpse of the jet-set lifestyle and the conscience-deficient mind-set of the aggressive mass-tort specialists" (Pate). Still others called *The King of Torts* enjoyable, saying the novel "is a quick and absorbing read; perfect for a plane ride or a leisurely day, and just the kind of book readers have come to expect . . . from Grisham" (Singhania). It has a "crisp, accessible style," as it details how "a good-hearted young lawyer falls into a moral sinkhole" (Donohue).

Several critics commented positively on the story itself, mentioning the "considerable fascination" of watching "Carter amass vast wealth, a Gulfstream jet, a Georgetown house, a Caribbean villa, even as we know his downfall is inevitable" (Anderson). They also feel that Carter's "downfall is brilliantly handled," adding that watching Grisham in this novel is like "watching a footballer coming back to form" (Dugdale).

Some reviews mention the novel's humor, an attribute most readers don't associate with Grisham. According to one, Grisham is "clearly anxious to be more than a mere story-teller, [and] has now grasped how to infuse satire into the legal thriller." *The King of Torts,* the reviewer claimed, "is [Grisham's] first successful realization of that new recipe" (Dugdale).

Other positive assessments have included "an unexpectedly enjoyable ride" (Millar), a "pageturningly compulsive" read (Brett), "a frisky improvement over Grisham's last couple of lawyer stories" (Kirschling), and a book that shows off the "pacing and skills of a natural storyteller" (Brett).

On the negative side, a few reviewers feel that *The King of Torts* "fails to convince" (Grimwood). They persist in wishing for better dialogue and real people to care about. One observed, "The book's main flaw is Grisham's failure to flesh out his characters. Even after 372 pages, it's difficult to visualize Carter or understand his motivations. Depictions of characters that should add depth to Carter, such as his father, do little to help. Instead, there's a sense of remoteness, as though the reader is just watching rather than feeling, the story" (Singhania).

10

Recent Books by John Grisham

John Grisham's most recent works include three novels, *The Bleachers* (2003), *The Last Juror* (2004), and *The Broker* (2005), as well as a real-life crime account, *The Innocent Man* (2006), a story Grisham became interested in because it involved a mentally ill man in danger of being put to death for a crime he didn't commit. Each of the discussions in this chapter contains a brief summary of plot and theme, ending with a synthesis of early critical reactions to the book.

BLEACHERS

Not treated in detail in *Revisiting John Grisham* is Grisham's sixteenth novel, *Bleachers*, published, like *The King of Torts*, in 2003. In *Bleachers*, a short novel, Grisham focuses nostalgically on protagonist Neely Crenshaw of Messina, Mississippi, a former high school football quarterback, an All-American whose prospects for a professional career end with a college knee injury. After years of aimless post-football meandering (he's now selling houses in Orlando, Florida), Neely returns to Messina for four days one October to stand vigil as his former high school football coach, Eddie Rake, lies dying. Neely brings with him a load of conflicted feelings about Rake, whose winning record on the playing fields is blemished by a losing record of behavior toward his players. Rake has been cruelly demanding of the boys who trained with him, long ago letting one 15-year-old die of heat prostration during a rigorous workout.

Bleachers is about reunion and fruitless dreams. Eddie Rake's ex-students gather in the bleachers at the old stadium (now called Rake Field) and drink beer while sitting deathwatch for their former teacher. The novel gets its title from this setting as well as from one of Rake's grueling exercises: his teams had to repeatedly run up and down the stadium's tiered stairs. Side plots focus on a mystery related to the 1987 high school championship and on Neely's efforts to rekindle a romance with a girlfriend he dumped in high school for another who, as the saying went in those days, put out.

Among Grisham's non-law-related books, *Bleachers* ranks between *A Painted House* and *Skipping Christmas*. It lacks the beauty and earnest effort at characterization offered up in *A Painted House*, but it is nevertheless more substantial than his holiday trifle, *Skipping Christmas*. Like *A Painted House*, *Bleachers* has autobiographical content. Grisham was, after all, an occasional quarterback at his own high school in Southhaven, Arkansas. However, despite Grisham's firsthand experiences with the issues, the novel's plot, especially its ending, seems strangely threadbare.

In fact, many works have treated the same or similar topics. Pat Conroy's *My Losing Season* tells a more brutal version of Grisham's *Bleachers*, with a sadder, perhaps more realistic ending. Edward Albee's play *All Over* describes a death vigil, this one kept for a family patriarch. There is also, of course, *As I Lay Dying*, published in 1930 by Grisham's fellow Mississippi author William Faulkner. Detailing the death and burial of one Addie Bundren, it is an American classic.

As for themes, "You can't go home again" is one, already done beautifully by Thomas Wolfe in a novel by that name. Another theme is that victory (and achieving manhood despite the tyranny of adults) comes at a cost (e.g., *Junction Boys: How Ten Days in Hell with Bear Bryant Forged a Championship Team* by Jim Dent) and athletic fame is fleeting (A.E. Housman's "To an Athlete Dying Young") and destructive (Jason Miller's play, *That Championship Season*). Certainly, *Bleachers* contributes to discussions about the questionable value of high-powered high school athletics and contains a storyline and themes that many interested in the ethics of sports and perhaps school-age readers can especially appreciate.

THE LAST JUROR

Grisham's seventeenth novel, *The Last Juror* (2004), returns readers to Clanton, Mississippi, a make-believe town set in fictional Ford County where Grisham situated his first novel, *A Time to Kill*. According to an online Barnes and Noble interview with the author, Grisham began *The Last Juror* soon after finishing *A Time to Kill* in 1989, even reprising some of its characters. He put the project on the back burner, however, when *The Firm*, his second novel and legal thriller *par excellence*, soared to best-sellerdom. "Do what sells" was Grisham's writing motto, and for the next several years, he obeyed that dictum.

In 2003 Grisham returned to the 100 pages or so that would become *The Last Juror*. Covering a period of 10 years, from 1970 to 1979, *The Last Juror* tells the story of Joyner William Traynor, a 23-year-old journalism major and college dropout who moves south from his home in Memphis to Clanton, where, thanks to a loan from his wealthy grandmother, he takes over Clanton's newspaper, the *Ford County Times*. At about the same time, a brutal rape and stabbing occurs in Clanton, the victim a young mother whose two small children witness the crime. Arrested for murder is Danny Padgitt, a ne'er-do-well member of a redneck crime family that makes its money from moonshine, robbery, gambling, prostitution, and marijuana. A jury finds Danny guilty but spares him execution.

Miss Callie Ruffin serves on that jury. She is the last juror to be picked for the trial (thus the novel's title) and the first black person ever to serve in such a capacity in Ford County. Over the nine years that Danny Padgitt is in jail, readers get to know Miss Callie through her increasingly warm friendship with Traynor, who is nicknamed Willie by the locals as they grow ever fonder of him. There is reason to worry about Miss Callie because Danny, as he is led off to prison, threatens the jury: "You convict me, and I'll get every damned one of you" (156). When he is inexplicably released on parole in 1979 and jurors start dying, fears mount that Miss Callie will be harmed.

The Last Juror fared especially well with critics and for good reason. They rated it among Grisham's best novels in part because Grisham fleshes out both of his main characters—Willie (he has long hair and drives a Triumph Spitfire) and Miss Callie (six of her seven children are college professors, and Grisham even includes her recipe for pot roast)—causing readers to genuinely care about them as human beings, not just as vehicles driving plot. Grisham also deserves (and gets) praise for his rendering of 1970s Mississippi, tracing as he does changes in small-town race relations and the economic shift from mom-and-pop stores downtown to suburban Wal-Mart–style shopping. Even so, he manages to avoid too much heavy philosophizing, keeping his focus squarely on the people and the physical details of a place he plainly loves. And he doesn't merely rhapsodize; he writes honestly about the South's good and not-so-good qualities.

THE BROKER

Grisham's eighteenth novel, *The Broker,* appeared in January of 2005, surprising readers with its focus on international intrigue. The protagonist this time around is more of an antihero than a hero. His name is Joel Backman; he is "the broker" of the novel's title, and although he is an attorney and a lobbyist, he has gained notoriety as a spy. Convicted of trying to sell a Pakistani-created software program that would disable surveillance satellites, he is shipped off to prison before the novel begins. Suddenly, after serving six years of a 20-year sentence, he finds himself on the streets again, pardoned by the President of the United States, who is about to leave office.

But the streets he finds himself on are not in the United States. Because the CIA wants to learn more about the satellite system Backman is linked to, Teddy Maynard—Grisham's CIA director resurrected from *The Brethren*—decides to use Backman as a decoy. In an inverted version of a witness-protection program, the CIA none too secretly deposits Backman in Italy, in the northern cities of Treviso and then Bologna, in hopes that those who are involved in the satellite scheme will try to silence him. With that goal in mind, the CIA leaks his name and location. Soon, assassins are closing in, with Backman eluding not only them but also the CIA agents presumably there to protect him.

Once Backman arrives in Italy and is hiding behind the pseudonym Marco Lazzeri, the novel becomes as much travelogue as spy thriller. Like Marco, readers are treated to language lessons (Marco doggedly studies Italian, eventually with an alluring tutor and love interest Francesca Ferro), strolls around romantic piazzas, tours of churches and basilicas, art exhibits featuring frescoes and statuary, and descriptions of coffee houses and countless pasta dinners (Grisham admits to gaining 10 pounds while researching the novel). The only drawback for Backman is he must evade not only the foreign operatives who would kill him, but also the CIA agents who want information that they can best get if he is dead.

Grisham's *The Broker* was nearly as well received as his previous novel, *The Last Juror.* Although some readers felt Grisham trod too far outside what could be considered his comfort zone (legal thrillers), others admired him for daring to extend his writing reach into politics and spying. In an afterword, Grisham, ever self-deprecating, acknowledges he is technologically out of his depth in *The Broker,* confessing, "My background is law, certainly not satellites or espionage. I'm more terrified of high-tech electronic gadgets today than a year ago. . . . It's all fiction, folks. I know very little about spies, electronic surveillance, satellite phones, smart-phones, bugs, wires, mikes, and the people who use them. If something in this novel approaches accuracy, it's probably a mistake." But none of that seems to matter to Grisham fans. They expect their man to delight them by changing up aspects of each novel, and he rarely disappoints them.

In *The Broker*, Grisham explores new ground in other ways as well. Although parts of *The Partner* and *The Testament* are set outside the United States (Brazil), *The Broker* goes considerably beyond either one in explor-ing a new geography. Grisham clearly loves northern Italy, and he com-municates his passion through sensuous writing and, in places, pleasantly languorous pacing.

With his novel's protagonist, Grisham continues a trend. Joel Backman joins other less-than-admirable Grisham lead characters—Clay Carter (*King of Torts*), Ray Atlee (*The Summons*), and Josh Stafford (*The Testa-ment*)—who, though selfish and insensitive at the beginning of their respective stories, may (or may not) develop a degree of character and compassion by the end. When *The Broker* gets underway, Backman has divorced his third wife and is despised by at least two of his three children. Even Backman himself admits to having lived a "sloppy life." Grisham seems to believe it matters whether a man like Backman becomes even a slightly better person.

THE INNOCENT MAN

Grisham's *The Innocent Man*, published in October 2006, is his foray into nonfiction writing. The book tells the story of Ronald Keith Williamson, a baseball player who grew up in the 1950s and 1960s in the small town of Ada, Oklahoma. Drafted by the Oakland Athletics in 1971, Williamson moved west with dreams of mounting a successful major league career. Injuries, poor behavior, and early signs of bipolar disorder brought him home six years later. He was in Ada in 1982 when a young woman by the name of Debra Sue Carter, a waitress, was raped and strangled in her home, her body decorated with ketchup. Following an investigation of several years, Williamson and a friend, science teacher Dennis Fritz, were arrested for the crime. A fellow prisoner had said that while in jail on an unrelated charge, Williamson had confessed to the murder. Williamson and Fritz were tried separately in 1988 and both were found guilty. Fritz received life imprisonment, and Williamson found himself on death row.

Eleven years of prison hell followed: life in a cave-like, underground holding area where guards taunted Williamson, whose mental illness complicated what was already a tortured life. Just five days before Williamson's scheduled execution, a public defender filed suit on his behalf on grounds that he had received poor counsel. He was granted a new trial, and this time, DNA evidence cleared both Fritz and Williamson. In fact, DNA tests showed a positive match against the first trial's chief witness. Free at last in 1999, Williamson struggled to put together a life outside of prison, but never quite successfully. He died on December 4, 2004, of cirrhosis of the liver.

One reason why Grisham reportedly became interested in Williamson's story is because of parallels between his life and Williamson's. In a *USA Today* review of *The Innocent Man*, Grisham says, "I grew up in a small town like Ada. I was born in Arkansas three hours from where Ron grew up. I lived in small towns in Arkansas and Mississippi where life revolved around Little League. We play ball all summer long. Nights, weekends, that's what we did. We both grew up in really strict homes, memorized Scripture, and you never missed church for anything."

Fascinated with the case, Grisham set to work researching. Over several months "he interviewed more than 100 people, including Williamson's sisters, Annette and Renee, plus Fritz and several other local men who had been wrongfully convicted of terrible crimes. He spoke with judges, lawyers and baseball coaches. He made numerous trips to Ada and visited Williamson's home for 11 years: death row at the Oklahoma state prison at McAlester" (Memmott).

To date, readers have generally praised *The Innocent Man*, according to metacritic.com, a Web site that keeps data on public responses to new and notable books.

In fact, general readers have so far assigned the book higher scores than reviewers did (8 out of 10 points compared to a 60 out of 100), praising Grisham for intervening in a situation where injustice and suffering would otherwise have prevailed and for applying his "amazing imagination" to a new kind of writing. Among newspaper reviews mentioned on metacritic.com, the *Boston Globe* accorded strong praise to *The Innocent Man*, calling it "every bit as suspenseful and fast-paced as his best-selling fiction." *Entertainment Weekly* labeled it Grisham's "strongest legal thriller yet, all the more gripping because it happens to be true." The *Daily Telegraph* stated that the book reported "not merely a 'miscarriage of justice' but its utter collapse," and the *Washington Post* observed that Grisham's reasoning in the book "is sound and his passion is contagious" (http://www.metacritic.com/books/authors/grishamjohn/innocentman#critics).

Other reviewers offered less positive reactions. Janet Maslin of the *New York Times* labeled *The Innocent Man* "less spectacular than sturdy," and the *Chicago Tribune* observed that Grisham writes with "such restraint that . . . he fails to arouse sufficient anger at the miscarriage Williamson and Fritz suffered." Meanwhile, the reviewer for the *Los Angles Times* claimed *The Innocent Man* lacks "historical context," and the *Wall Street Journal* critic stated that Grisham's presentation of the legal issues is "oversimplified."

Bibliography

BOOKS BY JOHN GRISHAM

A Time to Kill. New York: Bantam Doubleday Dell, 1989.
The Firm. New York: Bantam Doubleday Dell, 1991.
The Pelican Brief. New York: Bantam Doubleday Dell, 1992.
The Client. New York: Bantam Doubleday Dell, 1993.
The Chamber. New York: Doubleday, 1994.
The Rainmaker. New York: Doubleday, 1995.
The Runaway Jury. New York: Doubleday, 1996.
The Partner. New York: Doubleday, 1997.
The Street Lawyer. New York: Doubleday, 1998.
The Testament. New York: Doubleday, 1999.
The Brethren. New York: Doubleday, 2000.
A Painted House. New York: Doubleday, 2001.
Skipping Christmas. New York: Doubleday, 2001.
The Summons. New York: Doubleday, 2002.
The King of Torts. New York: Doubleday, 2003.
Bleachers. New York: Doubleday, 2003.
The Last Juror. New York: Doubleday, 2004.
The Broker. New York: Doubleday, 2005.
The Innocent Man. New York: Doubleday, 2006.

MEDIA ADAPTATIONS

Motion Pictures

The Firm. Dir. Sydney Pollack, Paramount Pictures, 1993, Based on the novel.

The Pelican Brief. Dir. Alan J. Pakula. Warner Bros., 1993. Based on the novel.

The Client. Dir. Joel Schumacher. Warner Bros., 1994. Based on the novel.

The Chamber. Dir. James Foley. Universal Pictures, 1996. Based on the novel.

A Time to Kill. Dir. Joel Schumacher. Warner Bros., 1996. Based on the novel.

The Rainmaker. Dir. Francis Coppola. Constellation Films, 1997. Based on the novel.

The Gingerbread Man. Dir. Robert Altman. Enchanter Entertainment, 1998. Story by John Grisham.

A Painted House. Dir. Alfonso Arau. Hallmark Hall of Fame Productions and CBS-TV, 2003. Based on the novel.

Runaway Jury. Dir. Gary Fleder. New Regency Pictures, 2003. Based on the novel.

The Street Lawyer. Dir. Paris Barclay. Touchstone Television and ABC-TV, 2003. Based on the novel.

Mickey. Dir. Hugh Wilson. Mickey Productions, 2004. Original screenplay by John Grisham.

Christmas with the Kranks. Dir. Joe Roth. Skipping Christmas Productions, 1492 Pictures, and Revolution Studios, 2004. Based on the novel *Skipping Christmas*.

TELEVISION SHOWS

The Client. 1995–96. Based on the movie and novel.

GENERAL WORKS ABOUT JOHN GRISHAM

Arnold, Martin. "Now, Grisham by E-mail." *New York Times*, 29 January 1998: B9.

Black, Joel. "Grisham's Demons." *College Literature* 25, no. 1 (Winter 1998): 35–40.

Brown, Ed. "Grisham's High Ground." *Fortune* 136, no. 5 (16 March 1998): 48.

Diggs, Terry K. "Through a Glass Darkly: John Grisham and Scott Turow Lay Down the Law for Millions of Americans: Just What Is It They're Trying to Tell Us?" *ABA Journal* 82 (October 1996): 72–75.

Evain, Christine. "John Grisham's Megabestsellers." *Subverted Codes and New Structures*. Eds. Francois Gallix and Vanessa Guignery. Paris: PU de Paris-Sorbonne, 2004.

Goodnight, G. Thomas. "The Firm, the Park and the University: Fear and Trembling on The Postmodern Trail." *The Quarterly Journal of Speech* 81, no. 3 (August 1995): 267–90.

"Grisham, John." *Current Biography* 54, no. 9 (September 1993): 21–24.

John Grisham: A Reader's Checklist and Reference Guide. Middletown, CT: CheckerBee Inc., 1999.

Martin, Terrence. "From Redskin to Redneck: Atrocity and Revenge in American Writing." *Comparative Literature and Culture: A WWWeb Journal* 3, no. 2 (June 2001): n.p.

Nickelson, Katie. "Lawyers as Tainted Heroes in John Grisham's Novels." *The Image of the Hero in Literature, Media, and Society.* Ed. Steven Kaplan. Pueblo, CO: Colorado State University Press, 2004.

Nolan, Tom. "John Grisham Testifies." *Mystery Scene* 79 (Spring 2003): 12–18.

Pringle, Mary Beth. *John Grisham: A Critical Companion.* Westport, CT: Greenwood, 1997.

Robson, Peter. "Adapting the Modern Law Novel: Filming John Grisham." *Journal of Law and Society* 26(1) (March 2001): 147–63.

Runyon, Randolph Paul. "John Grisham: Obsessive Imagery." *Southern Writers at Century's End.* Eds. Jeffrey J. Folks and James A. Perkins. Lexington: University of Kentucky Press, 1997, pp. 44–59.

Zaleski, Jeff. "The Grisham Business." *Publishers Weekly* 245, no. 3 (19 January 1998): 248–51.

INTERNET RESOURCES

John Grisham. Academy of Achievement Web site. http://www.achievement.org/autodoc/page/gri0pro-1

John Grisham. Biography and book information from Bantam-Doubleday. http://www.randomhouse.com/features/grisham/main.php

John Grisham: Biography and Much More. Answers.com Web site. http://www.answers.com/topic/john-grisham

John Grisham: Information on MSU's Most Famous Author. Grisham information from Mississippi State University. http://library.msstate.edu/grisham_room

John Grisham: Mississippi Writer's Page. http://www.olemiss.edu/depts/english/ms-writers/dir/grisham_john/

John Grisham Online. Fan site. http://www.randomhouse.com/features/grisham/main.php

WORKS CITED IN CHAPTERS

Introduction

USA Today. "Grisham," 30 June 1992: D5.

Biography of John Grisham

Agovino, Michael J. "A Magazine Lives, and Moves, On." Web Exclusive. John Grisham Web site. http://www.randomhouse.com/features/grisham

Jones, Malcolm, Ray Sawhill, and Corie Brown. "Grisham's Gospel." *Newsweek,* 15 February 1999: 65.

Kornbluth, Jesse. "'At Some Point in Life Everyone Thinks about Running Away': An Interview with John Grisham." *The Book Report* (February 1997), http://www.bookpage.com/9702bp/grisham/grishaminterview.html

Simon, Scott. "Interview: John Grisham Discusses His New Book *The King of Torts*." *Weekend Edition Saturday.* National Public Radio. 15 February 2002.

Summer, Bob. "Grisham's Southern Loyalists." *Publishers Weekly*, 3 March 2003: 33.

Victory, Richard. "Conspiracies of Gold." *Washingtonian* (June 1988): 37.

Wertheimer, Linda. "Interview: John Grisham Talks about His Latest Novel *A Painted House*." *All Things Considered.* National Public Radio. 6 February 2001.

The Partner, 1997

Amidon, Stephen. "Writing by Numbers." *London Sunday Times*, 23 March 1997, Features Section.

Dirck, Joe. "Grisham's Plot Taut; Characters Flabby." *Cleveland Plain Dealer*, 4 March 1997: 8E.

Donahue, Deirdre. "Grisham Repeats Himself in 'Partner.'" *USA Today*, 26 February 1997: 1D.

Dyer, Richard. "The Plot Thickens in Grisham's Latest." *Boston Globe*, 3 March 1997: C6.

Giffin, Glenn. "Penning the Perfect Crime: Grisham's Clever Lawyer Salts Away $90 Million in Intricate *The Partner*." *Denver Post*, 27 February 1997: E12.

Goodrich, Lawrence J. "Grisham's Morality Tale in a World without Morality." *Christian Science Monitor*, 26 March 1997: 13.

Holt, Patricia. "The Trail Goes Cold for Grisham." *San Francisco Chronicle*, 3 March 1997: E3.

Kelly, Katy. "Grisham's Good Works Pay Off in the Idea for 'Partner.'" *USA Today*, 27 February 1997: 7D.

Kisor, Henry. "Wired for Suspense; Grisham's Latest Hits Right Buttons." *Chicago Sun-Times*, 26 February 1997: 45.

Kornbluth, Jesse. "Interview with John Grisham." *The Book Report.* AOL. 12 February 1997. www.bookreporter.com/authors/au-grisham-john.asp.

Marcus, Greil. "An Anthem of Disillusion: My Country 'Tis of Whom?" *New York Times*, 9 February 1997: E2.

Maryles, Daisy. "Behind the Bestsellers." *Publishers Weekly*, 10 March 1997: 18.

"*The Partner*; Book Reviews." *Publishers Weekly*, 10 February 1997: 69.

Pate, Nancy. "Lawyer on the Lam: Grisham's *The Partner* More Cynical Caper than Courtroom Thriller." *Arizona Republic*, 13 April 1997: F12.

Rotenberk, Lori. "Great Expectations for *The Partner*." *Chicago Sun-Times*, 26 February 1997: 45.

Singer, Dale. "John Grisham's Latest Legal Book Lacks the Typical Fire." *St. Louis Post-Dispatch*, 15 March 1997: 33.

Twain, Mark. *Huckleberry Finn*. New York: Penguin, 2002, p. 368.

Warmbold, Carolyn Nizzi. "Mover, Shaker, Thriller: Grisham's Latest Delivers." *Atlanta Journal and Constitution*, 26 February 1997: 1D.

Woog, Adam. "Will *The Partner* Be a Firm Success?" *Seattle Times*, 16 March 1997: M2.

The Street Lawyer, 1998

Baldacci, Leslie. "Law of the Street; Grisham's Latest Is a Refuge for Homeless." *Chicago Sun-Times*, 4 February 1998: 45.

Donahue, Deirdre. "Grisham's *Street Lawyer* Goes Begging." *USA Today*, 4 February 1998: 1D.

Dyer, Richard. "Grisham's Lawyer Not a Total Loss." *Boston Globe*, 10 February 1998: E1.

Heybach, Rene. "World of Street Lawyer Looks Different to a Front Line Advocate." *Chicago Sun-Times*, 15 February 1998: Show 4.

Holt, Patricia. "Grisham Goes to Bat for Homelessness: Street Lawyer Defends Them." *San Francisco Chronicle*, 4 February 1998: E1.

Kakutani, Michiko. "Books of the Times; A Lawyer Converts to Virtue." *New York Times*, 10 February 1998: E1.

Millar, Peter. "Easy Writer." *London Times*, 21 March 1998: Features.

Ogle, Connie. "The Street Lawyer." *Miami Herald*, 12 February 1998: n.p.

Pate, Nancy. "The Street Lawyer." *Orlando Sentinel*, 2 February 1998: n.p.

Petit, Chris. "Books Spring Fiction: A Brief Refused." *Guardian*, 26 March 1998: 10.

Sutherland, John. "Million-Dollar Lawyer." *London Sunday Times*, 22 March 1998: Features.

The Testament, 1999

Bell, Bill. "*The Testament* by John Grisham." *New York Daily News*, 10 February 1999: n.p.

Berlins, Marcel. "Where Are the Thrills?" *London Sunday Times*, 31 January 1999: Features.

Berthel, Ron. "New Novel a Testament to Grisham's Storytelling Skills." *BC Cycle*, 1 March 1999: Lifestyle.

Donahue, Deirdre. "The Testament by John Grisham." *Chicago Sun-Times*, 3 February 1999: 38.

Dyer, Richard. "In New Grisham, More Plotting." *Boston Globe*, 9 February 1999: D1.

Holman, Hugh C., and William Harmon. *A Handbook to Literature*, 6th ed. New York: Macmillan, 1992.

"Mr. Burns Quotes." Humorsphere. http://www.humorsphere.com/simpsons/mr-burns-quotes.htm

O'Brien, Sean. "Books; Thrills Go Missing in the Jungle." *Guardian*, 20 February 1999: 10.

Pate, Nancy. "*The Testament* by John Grisham." *Orlando Sentinel*, 5 February 1999: x.

"Twentieth-Century American Bestsellers." University of Illinois Graduate School of Library and Information Science. http://www3.isrl.uiuc.edu/~unsworth/courses/bestsellers/search.cgi?title=The+Testament

The Brethren, 2000

Abrams, M. H. *A Glossary of Literary Terms*, 6th ed. Fort Worth: Harcourt, 1993.

Connelly, Sherryl. "John Grisham Gets Frisky." *New York Daily News*, 6 February, 2000: 19.

Donahue, Deirdre. "Grisham's Droning Brethren a D.C. Drag." *USA Today*, 1 February 2000: 1D.

Dyer, Richard. "With a Blundering Plot, Grisham's *Brethren* Is Relatively Feeble," *Boston Globe*, 9 March 2000: F4.

Galarneau, Andrew Z. "Grisham's Thriller Is More of Same—Sure to Please His Fans." *Buffalo News*, 27 February 2000: 6H.

Goodman, Walter. "Legal Thriller Obeys Laws of Commerce." *New York Times*, 29 February 2000: E1.

Harris, Michael. "Cynicism Infiltrates Grisham's World." *Los Angeles Times*, 15 February 2000: E3.

Heller, Helen. "Wanted: Blockbuster Editor's Heading Goes Here." *Toronto Star*, 13 February 2000: Entertainment.

Kipen, David. "Grisham Rushes in Where Clancy Treads." *San Francisco Chronicle*, 3 February 2000: B1.

Larson, Susan. "Pardon Me, Boys." *New Orleans Times-Picayune*, 6 February 2000: D7.

Mabe, Chauncey. "Grisham to Try Serialized Novel in the Court of Reader Opinion." *Columbus Dispatch*, 10 January 2000: 7B.

O'Briant, Don. "Net Site Offers Preview of Grisham's Brethren." *Atlanta Constitution*, 20 January 2000: 2D.

Sandstrom, Karen. "Grisham Delivers Plot, Not Strong Characters; Tale of Politics, Corruption and Greed Lacks Depth." *Cleveland Plain Dealer*, 1 February 2000: 1E.

Singer, Dale. "Shady Characters Are Up to Their Old Tricks in Grisham's Latest." *St. Louis Post-Dispatch*, 13 February 2000: F10.

Taylor, Andrew. "Monday Book: Master of the Blockbuster Is Hostage to Formula." *London Independent*, 7 February 2000: 5.

Thorne, Matt. "Anarchic, Surprising and Really Quite Crazy." *London Independent*, 30 January 2000: 11.

Tompkins, Jane P. "Sentimental Power: Uncle Tom's Cabin and the Politics of Literary History." In *The New Feminist Criticism: Essays on Women, Literature, and Theory*, Ed. Elaine Showalter. New York: Pantheon, 1985, pp. 81–104.

A Painted House, 2000

Berthel, Ron. "No Lawyers, No Judges, No Juries—No Foolin'!" *Associated Press*, 12 February 2001: Lifestyle.

Bolt, Ranjit. "Trouble Comes to the Cotton Fields." *London Spectator*, 10 March 2001: 42.

Crosbie, Lynn. "Grisham's Idyll." *Toronto Star*, 11 February 2001: BK01.

Dugdale, John. "What? No Lawyers?" *London Sunday Times*, 28 January 2001: Features.

Dyer, Richard. "Grisham Returns to Roots in Novel Departure." *Boston Globe*, 24 April 2001: Living E5.

Kinsella, Bridget. "You Can Go Home Again; In His Upcoming Novel, John Grisham Takes a Risk and Leaves the Lawyers Behind." *Publishers Weekly*, 22 January 20 2001: 178.

Maslin, Janet. "Watching Grass Grow and Men Fight." *New York Times*, 8 February 2001: E9.

Millar, Peter. "House Proud." *London Times*, 3 February 2001: Features.

Nebenzahl, Donna. "Grisham's Latest Has No Judges, Juries or Lawyers." *Montreal Gazette*, 3 February 2001: J3.

Slater, Joyce R. "Grisham without Benefit of Counsel." *Chicago Sun-Times*, 4 February 2001: Show 8.

Yanofsky, Joel. "Grisham Wants Respect." *Montreal Gazette*, 18 March 2001: J1.

Skipping Christmas, 2001

"Christmas with the Kranks." Rotten Tomatoes. http://www.rottentomatoes.com/m/Christmas_with_the_kranks/

Crosbie, Lynn. "A Christmas Tale." *Toronto Star*, 25 November 2001.

Fretts, Bruce. "Yule Primers; John Grisham, Jan Karon, and Jimmy Carter Earn Holiday Cheers (and Jeers) with Christmas Stories." *Entertainment Weekly*, 23 November, 2001: 72.

Guinn, Jeff. "*Skipping Christmas*: A Novel by John Grisham." *Fort Worth Star-Telegram*, 28 November 2001.

Kisor, George. "Christmas Ornaments for Their Authors' Dotage." *Chicago Sun-Times*, 18 November 2001: 14.

Lively, Adam. "What a Turkey." *London Sunday Times*, 18 November 2001: Features.

Mazmanian, Adam. "Books in Brief: Fiction and Poetry." *New York Times*, 23 December 2001: 17.

Minzesheimer, Bob. "Grisham Leaves Thrills Behind for 'Christmas.'" *USA Today*, 7 November 2001: 1D.

Nguyen, Lan N., Kyle Smith, Mike Neill, Michelle Tauber, Cynthia Sanz, Alec Foege, and V. R. Peterson. "Picks and Pans." *People*, 10 December 2001: 49.

Ogle, Connie. "*Christmas in Plains* by Jimmy Carter and *Skipping Christmas* by John Grisham." *Miami Herald*, 12 December 2001.

Pate, Nancy. "*Skipping Christmas* by John Grisham." *Orlando Sentinel*, 14 November 2001: n.p.

Roberts, Rex. "Ho, Ho, Ho." *News World Communications: Insight on the News*, 31 December 2001: 28.

Snyder, Blake. Review of *Christmas with the Kranks*. MovieWeb. http://www.movieweb.com/movies/reviews/review.php?film=2476#x0026;review=4435

Spencer, Charles. "A Dickens of a Story: Charles Spencer Enjoys John Grisham's Cheery Update of *A Christmas Carol*." *London Sunday Telegraph*, 16 December 2001: 16.

The Summons, 2002

Anderson, Patrick. "Heeding the Call of His Style." *Washington Post*, 28 January 2002: C03.

Donahue, Deirdre. "*Summons* Recalls Best of Grisham." *USA Today*, 31 January 2002: 1D.

Dugdale, John. "Is He Bored with Propping Up the Bar?" *London Sunday Times*, 10 February 2002: n.p.

Dyer, Richard. "In *Summons* Grisham Is on Familiar, but Not Firm Ground." *Boston Globe*, 12 February 2002: E6.

Guinn, Jeff. "*The Summons* by John Grisham." *Fort Worth Star–Telegram*, 13 February 2002: n.p.

Liptak, Adam. "Take the Money." *New York Times*, 24 February 2002: 13.

Maslin, Janet. "$3 Million Might Tempt Just about Any Lawyer." *New York Times*, 5 February 2002: 7.

Millar, Peter. "Inherited Trouble." *London Times*, 9 February 2002: Features.

Spencer, Charles. "The Root of All Evil." *London Sunday Telegraph*, 17 February 2002: 15.

Svetkey, Benjamin. "John Grisham's Latest Thriller Is Guilty of Forgettable Characters and a Lackluster Plot." *Entertainment Weekly*, 15 February 2002: 60.

The King of Torts, 2003

Anderson, Patrick. "John Grisham: Chasing the Ambulance Chasers." *Washington Post*, 3 February 2003: C01.

Appelo, Tim. "Books in Brief: Fiction." *New York Times*, 9 March 2003: 22.

Brett, Simon. "Grisham Props Up the Bar Yet Again." *London Daily Mail*, 7 February 2003: n.p.

Cogdill, Oline. "'The King of Torts' by John Grisham." *South Florida Sun Sentinel*, 5 March 2003: n.p.

Donahue, Deirdre. "'King' Dethrones Our Fealty to Easy Money." *USA Today*, 4 February 2003: 7D.

Dugdale, John. "The Lure of the Fat-Cat Life." *London Sunday Times*, 9 February 2003: 44.

Dyer, Richard. "Grisham Fall into Formula with 'Torts.'" *Boston Globe*, 25 February 2003: E6.

Grimwood, Jon Courtenay. "Thriller: A Lawyer unto Himself." *Guardian*, 22 February 2003: 29.

Grisham, John. "Interview: Grisham on Grisham." *Entertainment Weekly*, 2 February 2004.

Guinn, Jeff. "'The King of Torts' by John Grisham." *Fort Worth Star-Telegram*, 12 February 2003: n.p.

Kirschling, Gregory. "Laws of Motion; John Grisham's Latest Vehicle May Be Driven by Familiar Lawyers in Familiar Situations, but It's a Fast-paced Ride." *Entertainment Weekly*, 14 February 2003: 74.

Maslin, Janet. "Nice Young Lawyer; You Can Be a Legal Kingpin." *New York Times*, 3 February 2003: 7.

Millar, Peter. *The King of Torts. London Times*, 22 February 2003: 14.

Pate, Nancy. "'The King of Torts' by John Grisham." *Orlando Sentinel*, 5 February 2003: n.p.

Singhania, Lisa. "Grisham's New Thriller Provides Fast-Paced, if Predictable Entertainment." *Associated Press*, 10 March 2003: Lifestyle.

Recent Books by John Grisham

Maslin, Janet. "Grisham Takes on the Mystery of Reality." *New York Times*, 9 October 2006: n.p.

Memmott, Carol. "For Grisham, a New Turn into Non-fiction." *USA Today*, 10 October 2006: n.p.

Index

America Online (AOL), 7, 11

Associated Press reviews: *The Partner,* 13; *The Testament,* 42

Atlanta Constitution review, *The Partner,* 16

Barr, Nevada, 4

Bell, Bill, 42

Berthel, Ron, 13, 42

Bildungsroman, 70–71

Bleachers (Grisham), 5, 111–12

The Bonfire of the Vanities (Wolfe), serialization, 46

The Book Report (AOL), 7

Book signings: procedure, 4; at Square Books, 3–4

Boston Globe reviews: *The Brethren,* 56; *The Innocent Man,* 116; *The Summons,* 97; *The Testament,* 37

The Brethren (Grisham): *Boston Globe* review, 56; *Buffalo News* review, 56; character development, 49–50; critical reception, 55–57; *Daily News* review, 55; homophobia and, 52–53; *Independent* review, 55,

56; indirect advertising of, 46; on Liquid Audio, 45; literary, philosophical concepts, 53; *Los Angeles Times* review, 56; *Plain Dealer* review, 56; plot development, 50–52; plot summary, 46–49; politics of democracy in, 52; privacy and, 52; protagonist, 49; *San Francisco Chronicle* review, 56; *St. Louis Post-Dispatch* review, 55; thematic issues, 52–53; *Times-Picayune* review, 55–56; *USA Today* review, 56

The Broker (Grisham), 114–15

Buffalo News review, *The Brethren,* 56

Camus, Albert, 54

The Castle (Kafka), 54

Character development: *The Brethren,* 49–50; *King of Torts,* 103–5; *The Partner,* 10; *Skipping Christmas,* 77–78; *The Street Lawyer,* 23; *The Summons,* 89–91; *The Testament,* 35–37

Characters: *King of Torts,* 100–103, 105; *A Painted House,* 59, 64–66; *Skipping*

Christmas, 78–80; *The Street Lawyer*, 24–25; *The Summons*, 89–91; *The Testament*, 36

Chicago Sun-Times reviews: *The Street Lawyer*, 20, 27; *The Testament*, 37–39, 42

Chicago Tribune review, *The Innocent Man*, 116

Christian Science Monitor review, *The Partner*, 16

Christmas with the Kranks (movie), 83

The Client (Grisham), protagonist, 10

Conrad, Joseph, 41

Critics: Bell, 42; Berthel, 13, 42; Crosbie, 75; Donahue, 37–39, 42; Dyer, 37, 97; Heybach, 27; Holt, 17, 27–28; Maslin, 117; O'Brien, 43; Singer, 15; Spencer, 81

Crosbie, Lynn, 75

Daily News reviews: *The Brethren*, 55; *The Testament*, 42

Daily Telegraph review, *The Innocent Man*, 116

Donahue, Deirdre, 37–39, 42

Dostoyevsky, Fyodor, 53

Doubleday, marketing by, 7, 45, 59–60

Doubleday Book Club, 7

Dyer, Richard, 37, 97

Entertainment Weekly review, *The Summons*, 97

The Firm (Grisham), 54; protagonist, 10

The Green Mile (King), serialization, 46

Grisham, John: Baptist background, 3; Doubleday marketing, 7, 45, 59–60; early career, 2; early life, 1; existential themes, 53; family activities, 1–3; international appeal, 6; as Mississippi lawmaker, 2; on *New York Times* best-seller list, 2; *Oxford American* and, 4, 45, 60; readers and, 5; reading favorites, 2; recent books, 111–17; Square Books

and, 3–4; trial work, 3; Web site, 31; writing process for, 6; writing strengths, 25

Guardian review, *The Testament*, 43

Heart of Darkness (Conrad), 41

Hemingway, Ernest, 54

Heybach, Rene, 27

Holt, Patricia, 17, 27–28

Iles, Greg, 4

The Innocent Man (Grisham), 5–6, 115–17; *Boston Globe* review, 116; *Chicago Tribune* review, 116; *Daily Telegraph* review, 116; *Entertainment Weekly* review, 116; *Los Angeles Times* review, 116; Maslin's *New York Times* review, 117; *Wall Street Journal* review, 116

Joyce, James, 54

Kafka, Franz, 54

Kansas City Star review, *The Partner*, 17

King, Stephen, 46

The King of Torts (Grisham), 93; character development, 103–5; characters, 100–103; controversy, 106; critical reviews, 109–10; criticism, 104, 106–7; female characters, 105; friendship in, 109; good vs. evil in, 108–9; greed in, 109; humor in, 110; plot, 100–103; plot development, 105–7; power and corruption in, 108; prepublication, 99; pride in, 108; protagonist, 100, 103; secondary characters, 105; social, literary contexts, 107–8; thematic issues, 108; tort litigation treatment in, 99–100, 107

The Last Juror (Grisham), 112–14

Lawrence, D. H., 54

Liquid Audio, *The Brethren* on, 45

Literary Guild, 7

Los Angeles Times reviews: *The Brethren*, 56; *The Innocent Man*, 116

Malraux, Andre, 54
Maslin, Janet, 117
Miami Herald review, *The Street Lawyer*, 24
Mystery Guild, 7

New York Times best-seller list, 2
New York Times reviews: *The Innocent Man*, 117; *The Street Lawyer*, 23–24; *The Summons*, 96
Notes from the Underground (Dostoyevsky), 53

O'Brien, Sean, 43
Oxford American: Grisham's support of, 4; *A Painted House* serialization, 45, 60

A Painted House (Grisham): characters, 59, 64–66; class issues in, 67, 69–70; as coming-of-age tale, 71; Doubleday and, 59–60; filming of, 4; galley prints, 60; good life in, 72; and Grisham's childhood, 1–2; Mexican farmworker portrayal in, 66, 68; moral, spiritual growth in, 67; multiple plotlines, 67; nostalgia in, 68; online promotions, 60; *Oxford American's* serialization, 60; plot, 60–63; plot development, 66–67; poverty in, 68–69; print run, 59; publicity, 59–60; reviewers, 64, 66–67, 72–73; sales strategy, 60; setting, 67; social, cultural contexts, 68; strangers in, 67; subplot, 62; themes, 70–71
The Partner (Grisham), 7; American heroes and, 14–16; AOL and, 7, 11; *Atlanta Constitution* review, 16; Berthel's Associated Press review, 13; central question, 16; chapter organization, 12; character development, 10; *Christian Science Monitor* review, 16; *Denver Post* review, 16; among female readers, 15; Holt's *San Francisco Chronicle* review, 17; *Kansas City Star* review,

17; narrative perspective, 12–13; online reports, 17; plot, 8–10; plot development, 11–13; plot errors, plausibility, 13; print run, 7; *Publishers Weekly* review, 16; reviews, 13, 15–17; sales strategy, 7; *Seattle Times* review, 13; setting, 9; Singer's review, 15; social, literary contexts, 13–14; thematic issues, 14–16
Plain Dealer review, *The Brethren*, 56
Plot, plot development: *The Brethren*, 46–52; *King of Torts*, 100–103, 105–7; *A Painted House*, 60–63, 66–67; *The Partner*, 8–13; *Skipping Christmas*, 75–77, 80–81; *The Street Lawyer*, 20–23, 25–27; *The Summons*, 85–89, 91–93; *The Testament*, 32–35, 37–39
Protagonists: *The Brethren*, 49; *The Client*, 10; *The Firm*, 10; *King of Torts*, 100, 103; *Skipping Christmas*, 78; *The Summons*, 91; *The Testament*, 35
Publishers Weekly review, *The Partner*, 16

The Rainmaker (Grisham), 54
Recent books, 111–17; *Bleachers*, 111–12; *The Broker*, 114–15; *The Innocent Man*, 5–6, 115–17; *The Last Juror*, 112–14

San Francisco Chronicle reviews: *The Brethren*, 56; *The Partner*, 17; *The Street Lawyer*, 27–28
Sartre, Jean Paul, 54
Seattle Times review, *The Partner*, 13
Singer, Dale, 15
Skipping Christmas (Grisham): character development, 77–78; characters, 78–80; Christmas in, 82; critical responses, 83–84; Crosbie's *Toronto Star* review, 75; for female readers, 79; mindless materialism in, 82–83; movie version, 83; plot development, 80–81; plot summary, 75–77; protagonist, 78; reviews, 80–81; sales, 75; social, cultural contexts, 81; Spencer's *Sunday Telegraph*

review, 81; suburbia in, 81; themes, 82–83; third-person narrative in, 80; white, middle-class prejudices in, 81
Social, literary contexts: *King of Torts*, 107–8; *A Painted House*, 68; *The Partner*, 13–14; *Skipping Christmas*, 81; *The Street Lawyer*, 19, 27–28; *The Summons*, 93; *The Testament*, 39–41
Sony Pictures Entertainment, 83
Spencer, Charles, 81
Square Books signings, 3–4
St. Louis Post-Dispatch review, *The Brethren*, 55
The Street Lawyer (Grisham): celebrity trials and, 19; chapter organization, 26; character development, 23; cultural factors, 20; Heybach's *Chicago Sun-Times* review, 27; Holt's *San Francisco Chronicle* review, 27–28; *Miami Herald* review, 24; *New York Times* review, 23–24; opening scene, 25; plot, 20–23, 26; plot development, 25–27; plot plausibility, 27; popular reaction, 29; promotion, 19; research intrusiveness in, 26; reviews, 29–30; secondary characters, 24–25; social, historical contexts, 27–28; social issues in, 19; television project, 25; thematic issues, 28–29; weaknesses of, 23; wealth and power in, 28
The Summons (Grisham): character development, 89–91; characters, 89–91; circular structure, 91; critical responses, 96–97; Dyer's *Boston Globe* review, 97; *Entertainment Weekly* review, 97; father-son relationships in, 95; literary devices, 91–92; modern America in, 95; money in, 95; *New York Times* review, 96; plot, 85–89; plot development, 91–93; plot plausibility, 92–93; print run, 85; protagonist, 91; as quest novel, 94; responsibility in, 95; reviewers, 92; sales, 85; secondary characters, 91; setting, 93; sibling rivalry in, 95; social, literary

contexts, 93; *Sunday Telegraph* review, 97; *Sunday Times* review, 97; themes, 95–96; *USA Today* review, 96
The Sun Also Rises (Hemingway), 54
Sunday Telegraph reviews: *Skipping Christmas*, 81; *The Summons*, 97
Sunday Times reviews: *The Summons*, 97; *The Testament*, 36

The Testament (Grisham): Bell's *Daily News* review, 42; Berthel's Associated Press review, 42; chapter organization, 39; character development, 35–37; Donahue's *Chicago Sun-Times* review, 37–39, 42; Dyer's *Boston Globe* review, 37; *Heart of Darkness* and, 41; humor in, 35–36; narrative strands, 39; O'Brien's *Guardian* review, 43; opening, 38; optimistic message, 42; paperback sales, 32; plot, 32–35; plot development, 37–39; prepublication marketing, 31; print runs, 31; protagonist, 35; reviews, 36–39, 41–43; sales, 31–32; secondary characters, 36; setting, 37; social, historical, literary contexts, 39–41; *Sunday Times* review, 36; themes, 41–42; web promotion, 31
Themes: existential, 53; *A Painted House*, 70–71; *Skipping Christmas*, 82–83; *The Summons*, 95–96; *The Testament*, 41–42
Times-Picayune review, *The Brethren*, 55–56
Times review, *The Summons*, 97
A Time to Kill (Grisham), print run, sales, 2
The Trial (Kafka), 54
Turow, Scott, 6

USA Today reviews: *The Brethren*, 56; *The Summons*, 96

Waugh, Evelyn, 54
Williamson, Ronald Keith, 115–16
Wolfe, Tom, 46
Woolf, Virginia, 54

About the Author

MARY BETH PRINGLE is a Professor of English at Wright State University.

Critical Companions to Popular Contemporary Writers
First Series—*also available on CD-ROM*

V. C. Andrews *by E. D. Huntley*

Tom Clancy *by Helen S. Garson*

Mary Higgins Clark *by Linda C. Pelzer*

Arthur C. Clarke *by Robin Anne Reid*

James Clavell *by Gina Macdonald*

Pat Conroy *by Landon C. Burns*

Robin Cook *by Lorena Laura Stookey*

Michael Crichton *by Elizabeth A. Trembley*

Howard Fast *by Andrew Macdonald*

Ken Follett *by Richard C. Turner*

John Grisham *by Mary Beth Pringle*

James Herriot *by Michael J. Rossi*

Tony Hillerman *by John M. Reilly*

John Jakes *by Mary Ellen Jones*

Stephen King *by Sharon A. Russell*

Dean Koontz *by Joan G. Kotker*

Robert Ludlum *by Gina Macdonald*

Anne McCaffrey *by Robin Roberts*

Colleen McCullough *by Mary Jean DeMarr*

James A. Michener *by Marilyn S. Severson*

Anne Rice *by Jennifer Smith*

Tom Robbins *by Catherine E. Hoyser and Lorena Laura Stookey*

John Saul *by Paul Bail*

Erich Segal *by Linda C. Pelzer*

Gore Vidal *by Susan Baker and Curtis S. Gibson*